THE
INFORMATION
BROKERS

THE INFORMATION BROKERS

How to Start and Operate
Your Own Fee-Based Service

by Kelly Warnken

Information Management Series / 2

R. R. BOWKER COMPANY
New York & London, 1981

Published by R. R. Bowker Company
1180 Avenue of the Americas, New York, N. Y. 10036
Copyright © 1981 by Xerox Corporation
Printed and bound in the United States of America

Library of Congress Cataloging in Publication Data

Warnken, Kelly.
    The information brokers.

    (Information management series)
    Bibliography: p.
    Includes index.
    1. Information services—United States.
I. Title.   II. Series
Z674.5.U5W37   001.64'404   81-10170
ISBN 0-8352-1347-1   AACR2

CONTENTS

570343

PREFACE

Ever since I first published the *Directory of Fee-Based Information Services* in 1977, I have been beseiged by phone calls and letters from people requesting in-depth information on becoming an information broker. In the beginning, I answered every phone call and letter at length and in great detail, feeling that my background and experience qualified me to offer advice in this area. Like many owners and operators of fee-based information services, I have formal training as a librarian and practical experience (at the State University of New York, New Paltz), plus editorial knowledge (magazine work in San Francisco, audiovisual experience with public television in Chicago). In addition, I know first-hand the ins and outs, ups and downs of starting and operating a fee-based service; I began Information Alternative in 1977 and, although I do employ freelance help, it is still essentially a one-person operation.

The information requests continued and I continued to respond, feeling that at some point someone would write a book on the subject. When that happened, I thought, I will cut down on the length of my answers and merely respond with the bibliographic details of a single title.

In the years since 1977, interest in fee-based information services has increased; in fact, I am still answering inquiries at length. And no one has published a guide to starting and operating a fee-based service—which is why I wrote *The Information Brokers*. This practical, how-to guide explains the basics of setting up an information broker business and shows the reader how he or she can begin an operation. The potential entrepreneur, whether librarian, editor, businessperson, student, or whatever, is taken step-by-step through the process of becoming an information broker—from conducting an initial market study in the community, to setting up an office, to the all-important key to success, getting and keeping clients.

Working information brokers have provided input into all the chapters, but especially Chapters 9 and 10. These chapters are of particular importance to the prospective information broker in making a final decision. By reading If I Had It All to Do Again, the reader will learn, without risking failure, what does not work, as well as what does. Insights into the future of information brokering, where it appears to be headed, and where brokers hope it will go, are provided in Chapter 10, The Future.

Once you have read *The Information Brokers*, it is hoped you will refer to it again and again in the course of starting and operating a fee-based broker business. This guide is meant to be part of a process that includes market research, continuing education, and immeasurable amounts of plain hard work.

ACKNOWLEDGMENTS

The author wishes to thank the following people for their help in preparing this book: Tina Byrne (Regional Information and Communication Exchange); Robert Burgess (State University of New York at Albany, School of Library and Information Science); Rosemary Eakins (Research Reports); Barbara Whyte Felicetti (Info/motion); Sandra Ferguson (Legwork Writers Research Services); Andrew Garvin (FIND/SVP); Wayne Gossage (Gossage-Regan Associates); Richard S. Halsey (State University of New York at Albany, School of Library and Information Science); Ellen Boughn Henderson (After—Image, Inc.); Tim Knier (Knier Associates); Matthew Lesko (Washington Researchers); Judith Mahrer (Library Services); Moira Moore (SIS); Nigel Oxbrow (London Researchers); Jean Piety (Facts for a Fee); Marc Porat (Aspen Institute for Humanistic Studies); Martha Ammidon Powers; Melinda Scott (Peat, Marwick, Mitchell); Connie Steward (General Electric Company); Kathryn E. Taylor (Taylor & Associates); Robert Taylor (Syracuse University School of Information Studies); S. C. van der Valk (who compiled the Bibliography); Ty Webb (Info/Webb); and Celeste West (Booklegger Press).

YOU'RE GOING TO BE A WHAT?

This book will tell you how to start and operate a fee-based information service. While this bit of news may not send chills of excitement up and down the spine of the average person, it will at least be of interest to you. If you were not interested in starting and operating a fee-based information service—or at least in *thinking about* starting and operating one—there would be no reason to waste your time reading a book called *The Information Brokers*.

Actually, your reasons for wanting to start your own fee-based information service are immaterial and will not affect your chances for success in this field. How well you prepare yourself and how hard you work once you are afloat are most important.

The decision to go into this business is often made when circumstances necessitate a course of action. Retired librarians who find that a fixed income needs a little fixing may supplement their pensions by operating successful fee-based information services part-time. New library school graduates may turn to fee-based information services when the job of finding a job in a library becomes a dead-end career. One of the largest and most successful fee-based information services today was started by two women after graduation from library school. Or, when the mid-career librarian is about to be excessed, he or she begins to think about working independently. There may be other reasons, too; although to date most information services of this type have been started and operated by people with library or library school training, this is not a prerequisite to entering the field.

1

In any event, you feel—for whatever reasons—that it is time for a change, and starting a fee-based information service sounds good to you. You figure that you can be your own boss, make your own decisions, and certainly earn more money than you now earn.

To prepare yourself for this career change or beginning, you may have attended a conference on alternative careers for librarians, read *What Color Is Your Parachute*,[1] bought a book on starting your own business, and combed *Library Literature* for articles on information brokering.

And yet, you are still filled with questions. You do not feel you know everything you have always wanted to know about fee-based information services. You are not afraid to ask; you just do not know whom to ask. This book, coupled with further research you will be directed to undertake, should answer many of those questions.

Before we get into the nitty-gritty of how to operate a fee-based information service, let us look at a few definitions of what we are talking about.

Just what is a fee-based information service?

DEFINING THE TERMS

You have heard the terms before—fee-based information service, information broker, information consultant, freelance librarian, information specialist—and you are probably confused. What is the difference between an information broker and a freelance librarian? Is an information consultant an information specialist?

To set the record straight, fee-based information service includes corporate and institutional charge-back information services, privately owned fee-based information services, freelance librarians, information brokers, information consultants, information specialists, library consultants, information retailers, information-on-demand companies, researchers, freelance indexers, freelance catalogers, and others who provide library or information services for a fee.

Any of the following may describe the fee-based information service:

　　1. Services are provided for money.

2. The entity providing services may be a self-employed individual, a privately owned company with one or more employees, or a department of a business or institution, such as a library or university, run as a charge-back service.
3. A variety of clients are serviced; in the case of a department of a business or organization, outside as well as internal clients must be served.
4. Either library or information services may be provided.
5. A single service or any combination of services may be provided, but more than one source or supplier must be used. For example, a freelance cataloger provides a single service—cataloging—and may be considered a fee-based information service if he or she applies a variety of products and systems to an individual client's cataloging needs. A company that mass-produces a single cataloging system or product to solve a myriad of cataloging problems is not a fee-based information service.
6. There is no requirement as to time of operation; whether the service is operated full-time, part-time, seasonally, or year-round is irrelevant.

Now, let us examine the four kinds of fee-based information services—library or information consultant, information broker, freelance librarian, and single-function services.

A *library or information consultant* offers advice and is paid for that advice. The consultant's primary function is to make recommendations for solutions to problems, but in the course of advising a client, the consultant may actually be called on to provide solutions. For example, a library consultant who advises a client that the answer to information problems lies in the reorganization of an information collection may return to do the actual reorganizing.

An *information broker* provides information on demand, that is, research done on an hourly or contract basis, and, in theory, any or all of a long list of services (see list under Services later in this chapter), including consulting services.

A *freelance librarian* undertakes short-term jobs within a variety of information collections and normally works on the client's premises.

The *single-function service* includes freelance indexers and catalogers, and others whose titles are self-explanatory.

If it is all so simple, why does it seem so confusing? Confusion begins when the terms are misapplied. One midwestern information broker calls herself a freelance librarian, although she performs the tasks of an information broker and rarely works on site. One freelance librarian refers to herself as an information broker, but accepts only temporary short-term jobs within libraries.

When other terms are invented to describe fee-based information services, the situation is further complicated. If you look at the brochures of several such services, you will see such terms as information retailer, information-on-demand company, professional research business, and information-gathering company. Further adding to the confusion are arbitrary standards, such as that part-time businesses are excluded from the definition of fee-based information services, or that more than one person must be employed by a company.

Part of the reason for this confusion is that this is a young industry still developing, still trying to find its own identity. Even those people who have been in the profession for a number of years cannot seem to agree on what to call it. Andrew Garvin, founder of FIND/SVP, generally considered the front-runner in the field in America, says:

> This gets to be a little controversial. I've often said that I'm not sure there is an information broker industry. There have been a lot of definitions. . . . Is an information broker the same as a freelance librarian? Are an information broker and a freelance librarian the same as a freelance researcher? And is that the same as a consultant?[2]

If you think people within the fee-based information service field are confused, they are no more so than the people who use these services. Barbara Felicetti, owner of Info/motion in Lenox, Massachusetts, prefers to be called an information broker, but she uses the term "information specialist" with a potential client who may not understand what brokering is.[3]

Freelance librarian Martha Ammidon Powers finds that most people understand the term "freelance librarian" more easily than other terms. "However, some people don't really know what a freelance librarian does and imagine that I sit at home and send out overdue notices on my own!'"[4]

Felicetti maintains: "The terms aren't important to clients, but it might be useful for us if we could all agree on a single term. We're a young profession, but it's time for us to get serious and become recognized as a group."[5]

Recognition by the public is important, but perhaps it is too much to demand that this young profession agree on a single term. Other professions, however long established, use more than one term to describe their members—just ask your doctor or your physician, your attorney or lawyer. (Admittedly, however, each of those interchangeable terms is understood; not so, as yet, in fee-based information services.) The term you use to describe yourself should depend on your own preference, the services you offer, and what you feel your potential clients will best understand.

HISTORY IN BRIEF

SVP, for *s'il vous plait* (French for "if you please"), is generally considered the front-runner of the fee-based information services industry in Europe. Established in Paris during the 1940s, it provides to businesses that pay a monthly retainer answers to questions on all subjects of importance to companies and business owners. SVP now operates offices in several countries around the world, including Australia, Japan, Italy, England, and the United States. SVP's American affiliate, FIND/SVP, opened in the late 1960s and is owned and operated by Andrew Garvin, president, and Kathleen Bingham, executive vice president.

During the late 1960s to early 1970s, a few other companies began operating in North America—Information Resources, Information Access Corporation, Info/motion, and Inform, as well as dozens of individuals who moonlight at part-time fee-based information services while holding traditional library jobs.

In 1977, the *Directory of Fee-Based Information Services* (Information Alternative) listed 87 known fee-based information companies in the United States and Canada. The 1978–1979 edition added nearly 100 new services to that list, and the 1980–1981 directory included 257 services with a new section on services abroad. In addition, a bimonthly supplement published in the *Journal of*

Fee-Based Information Services (Information Alternative) lists between 10 and 20 new services in each issue.

Why the increase since 1977? The increase in the number of
services in recent editions of directories such as the *Directory of
Fee-Based Information Services* is due in part to increased awareness of existing services. It is often difficult to track down an
individual who operates a fee-based information service single-
handed, but through a variety of methods, including scanning
journals and other publications and calling library schools and
associations, fee-based information services are brought to the
attention of editors, and subsequently listed in directories.

Actual growth of the size of the fee-based information services
industry is due to a tight job market for librarians and an increase in
the amount of information available today. More and more librarians forced to seek jobs outside the traditional library setting
turn to operating fee-based information services as a solution to
unemployment. Many go out of business within a year or so, but
newly terminated librarians wait in the wings to take over after a
service fails.

If it were not for the tremendous growth of information in
recent years, however, there would be no market for fee-based
information services to serve. Today's information explosion has
created a need for a type of service that helps an individual or
company untrained in information-gathering techniques to cope
with the onslaught of data it faces each day. Twenty or 30 years ago,
it was not difficult to keep abreast of developments in a particular
field by subscribing to a few professional journals (perhaps even
reading them) and occasionally attending a conference (preferably
one held in a popular vacation spot). Today, it is much harder for
an individual or a company to keep pace with its own field without
the aid of a skilled professional or professional service to search,
abstract, and organize information into a wieldy package.

SERVICES

When strangers meet at a social gathering, the question "What do
you do for a living?" usually comes up fairly early in the conversation. It is a way of getting to know the other person quickly, a way
of sizing up someone in a hurry. The answers that people give to
that question are fairly easy to comprehend. We all know what

doctors, plumbers, teachers, secretaries, letter carriers, and mechanics do. But if you are an information broker, you are likely to hear "What in the world is that?"

In general, the information broker and fee-based information companies offer two types of services: gathering information and processing information. Specifically, these include all of the services in the following list. Do not be scared off by its length!

List of Services

Abstracting
Analyzing information
Appraising collections
Bibliographies
Cataloging
Clipping service
Computer software design
Consulting
Current awareness
Directories
Displays and exhibits for libraries
Document delivery
Editing
Editorial services
Evaluating information needs
Grants
Identifying experts
Indexing
Industry overview
Instant education
Literature searching
Loose-leaf updating
Maintenance of collections
Market research and survey preparation
On-line searching
Organizing collections
Part-time librarians and temporary replacement of librarians
Personnel selection
Photo and picture research
Programs for libraries

Public relations
Publishing
Purchasing service
Quick reference service
Records management
Repackaging information
Research
Résumés
Reviews
Selective dissemination of information
Seminars and workshops
Speakers service
Storytelling
Systems design
Thesaurus construction
Training
Translating
Verifying facts
Writing

If you are a librarian, you have already acquired most of the skills on this list and probably a few others. Perhaps you do not even recognize that you have some of these skills because you have always referred to them by another term or you have never stopped to identify as skills the tasks you routinely perform. Grabbing everything you can on a subject for somebody who needs to know something by tomorrow morning may be called reference work in the library, but it is "instant education" in the fee-based information services business. Still, it is the same thing, and you already know how to do it.

Read over the list of services again. Then prepare a list of skills you have acquired as a librarian (or other professional if you are not a librarian) through your current and previous jobs and/or those skills you were trained in at library (or other) school. Do not merely identify broad areas such as cataloging, reference, or acquisitions. Break each task into small steps, and you will see how many different skills you are capable of performing.

Once you become aware of the number of services you already provide clients (patrons), the idea of operating a fee-based information service will seem less threatening.

HOW LIBRARIES AND FEE-BASED INFORMATION SERVICES DIFFER

Comparing fee-based information services with libraries may not be like comparing apples with oranges, but it might be like comparing grapefruit with oranges. They are similar, but the differences outweigh the similarities.

A library, whether public, university, or special, serves a large but controlled group of patrons. A fee-based information service maintains far fewer clients, so must work very hard at finding new ones.

The user/provider relationships differ. A library can manipulate the intensity of service to its patrons depending on the size of staff it has available and the number of requests it must process at one time. On a busy night the reference librarian can limit the length of searches or merely point out the card catalog rather than spend a great deal of time with one patron at the expense of the rest. A fee-based information service is the client's hired hand, and each client expects its request answered and delivered on time, bar nothing.

Although both libraries and fee-based information services provide high-quality services, their functions are different. Take, for example, a request for information on the value of art deco bookends. The requesting library patron who receives help in locating books in the library collection, who is given an interlibrary loan, and who is referred to an appropriate association is a library patron well served. The fee-based information user who requests information on art deco bookends and receives a report that includes testimony by a recognized authority and an annotated bibliography on everything ever written about art deco bookends is a client well served.

Although the end results differ, both user and patron received what they expected—information on the value of art deco bookends.

There is room in the information world for both libraries and fee-based information services. As a few library administrators have discovered, there is room in some buildings for both a library and a fee-based information service. Jean Piety, head of the Cleveland Public Library's Facts for a Fee, began that fee-based information service in 1975 when she saw a need for both traditional library services and the in-depth research services that could be provided only by a fee-based industry. Public and university libraries in Minneapolis, Atlanta, Houston, and other American cities have followed suit.

ADVANTAGES AND DISADVANTAGES OF STARTING A SERVICE

Talking someone out of starting a fee-based information service is easy. Just mention that most small businesses fail. Or talk about the lack of job security. Bring up the irregular hours. Or remark on the loss of a regular paycheck.

But if talking someone out of starting a fee-based information service is easy, talking someone into it is even easier. Yes, small businesses do fail, but fee-based information services have enjoyed a lower failure rate than other small businesses. Perhaps it is because owners have avoided two often-mentioned reasons for business failures—undercapitalization and poor management.

Because a fee-based information service does not require the purchase of stock, lease of office space, or other substantial investment, it needs about the least amount of capitalization of any business. Although it is not advisable, some successful firms were started with no capitalization at all.

Librarians may not be trained in business management, but they clearly have an advantage over other potential owners when it comes to learning how to manage a business—they are accustomed to finding out about things they do not know by gathering information and taking continuing education courses.

Perhaps the fault librarians have here is overeducating themselves before taking the plunge into unfamiliar waters. While a prospective electrical contractor might shudder at the thought of plowing through government regulations and might never get around to actually reading those pamphlets from the Small Business Administration, the librarian has probably already scanned their tables of contents, skimmed through the text, photocopied relevant sections, filed the photocopies, and classified the file folders. On free evenings when the electrical contractor is designing a logo, the librarian is off taking a bookkeeping course to acquire confidence in setting up an accounting system.

As for lack of security—is that really so? If you are now a librarian, does your security depend on seeing the same faces day after day? On possibly losing a position due to budget cuts? On earning only slightly more than a nonprofessional?

But if there is a degree of insecurity on entering this new field, there is certainly no lack of freedom. You will gain the freedom to earn more money than most librarians, including administrators, freedom to choose your own hours, freedom to make your own decisions, freedom to experience challenges, and freedom to meet new people.

BASIC QUESTIONS AND ANSWERS

Q. What basic characteristics define a fee-based information service?

A. (1) Services are rendered for money; (2) business may be self-employed individual, privately owned company with many employees, or department of institution or business; (3) variety of clients; (4) may provide library or information services, a single service, or any combination of services.

Q. What are the four basic types of fee-based information services?

A. (1) Library or information consultant (gives advice and recommends solutions to problems, but may also provide the actual solutions); (2) information broker (researches on an hourly or contract basis); (3) freelance librarian (performs short-term jobs within a number of information collections); (4) single-function service (includes indexers, catalogers, and others).

Q. Is there agreement on a single term or description for this industry?

A. No. In this young, still developing industry, many descriptive terms overlap, and many people may be performing the same services under different titles.

Q. What is the oldest of the information broker services?

A. SVP is generally considered the front-runner. It was established in the 1940s in Paris. The U.S. affiliate, FIND/SVP, opened in the late 1960s.

Q. What accounts for the lower rate of business failure for fee-based information services compared to other small businesses?

A. The fee-based service requires relatively low capitalization, and librarians (who most often open these services) are already skilled in gathering information.

Q. What publications list operating fee-based information services?

A. *Directory of Fee-Based Information Services* lists U.S. and Canadian services, plus a section on services abroad; *Journal of Fee-Based Information Services* lists new services each issue.

NOTES

1. Richard Nelson Bolles, *What Color Is Your Parachute: A Practical Manual for Job-Hunters and Career-Changers* (Berkeley, Calif.: Ten Speed Press, 1972). Almost required reading for job hunters. Bolles conducts seminars based on his theory of the hidden job market.
2. "Profile," *Journal of Fee-Based Information Services* 1, no. 6 (November/December 1979): 13.
3. Ibid., no. 1 (January/February 1979): 5.
4. Ibid., no. 2 (March/April 1979): 4.
5. Ibid., no. 1 (January/February 1979): 5.

BEFORE
YOU
BEGIN

Do you have what it takes to start and operate a fee-based information service? More importantly, if you do not have it now, can you get it?

How do you find out what it takes? How wonderful it would be if instead of this chapter there appeared a checklist of qualities needed to be successful in this business. You could just run down the list and find out immediately if you are qualified to run such a service. If not, you need not waste any more of your time. If so, you could skip this, go on to the next chapter, and learn how to start your service.

Or it would be a simple decision if you could take a test that would determine how well you would do. Not one of those grueling essay tests, but just a short, quick quiz such as you find in the backs of magazines.

Unfortunately, there is no checklist and there is no quiz. There is, however, this chapter, and reading it is only a beginning. It will help you to identify necessary resources and provide guidelines to follow, but it cannot prepare you to open your business. That job is up to you.

Preparing yourself for opening day will take between 6 and 12 months, depending on how much time you devote to doing your homework. It may take even longer if you need to save money to open your business—pretty grim news, but a reality. Doing your homework will greatly minimize your risk of failure, however, so it is time well spent.

Before you begin, you will need to take stock of your skills. In addition to information-gathering skills, you must determine your ability to run a business. Operating a fee-based information service is no different from running any other type of business.

You must consider whether you will be able to find enough clients to keep you in business. By identifying potential clients before you begin, you can get an idea of the true need for a fee-based information service in your area.

And then there is money. How much money you will need to start will depend on your own financial circumstances. But to be sure, to start your business, you will need more money than you think you will need, and later on you will need even more.

TIME AND COMMITMENT

How much time will you devote to starting a fee-based information service? If you are already employed full time or going to school, you will have to confine your preparation to your free time, evenings, and weekends.

Take a look at how you now spend your free time. It is probably spent in a combination of daily chores that eat up large chunks of time, fulfilling responsibilities to other people, with a little left over for recreation.

What can you eliminate? Again, it is up to you. You could cut out recreation. You could hire a maid to free you from household chores. You could delegate responsibility to others.

If you find it impossible to gain more free time now, you may have to think twice about starting a fee-based information service—time is something you will need plenty of. For example, you must become familiar with every information resource in your area. That means paying an in-person visit to every library within driving distance. You will have to acquaint yourself with each general collection and know special holdings inside out so that you will not have to think twice about where to find information after you open your business.

While you are checking out libraries, learn the names of the library personnel. They are your future co-workers. Not knowing them or alienating them will only make life difficult for you once you get started. You will need to call on them frequently for help, and being on friendly terms is certainly an advantage.

On the other hand, if you are a librarian, do not expect any favors just because of that. You may, in fact, encounter hostility from those librarians who feel that charging for library services is unethical or unprofessional. However, you have as much right to use library facilities for your purposes as anyone else, provided you operate within library rules.

This is the time to find out those endless details. Does the copy machine make change? Is the library closed on Columbus Day? When is the best time to use data bases? Will the library be mobbed with students during exam times? Do not wait until you have an important client, a short deadline, and only a $10 bill to find out the answers to these and other questions.

Start a resource file on information collections that you plan to consult in the operation of your business. On index cards jot down details about each collection, including telephone number, hours of operation, individual names, and so on. Request copies of library handbooks and keep them in your pamphlet file.

Make contact with special libraries. Corporate librarians often moonlight for fee-based information services. Although you may not be able to use materials in-house, your contact can provide you with needed information.

Do not limit your investigation to libraries. Become familiar with all sources of information in your area. Find out what resources your local government offers. Talk to professors at nearby colleges. You may wish to contact them for an opinion in the future.

Once you are familiar with local sources, get to work on national information resources by plowing through directories of associations, businesses, and government in search of additions to your information resource file. Through literature, identify experts you can call on for information, experts in the business world, government, associations, and the academic world. Matthew Lesko of Washington Researchers maintains that "there is an expert for every subject."[1]

In other words, pull out all the stops. Pretend you have just hired yourself as a consultant. Your first task is to prepare a file of information sources to be used by a newly established fee-based information service. This will also be a good exercise in learning a new way of tackling an information problem. As a librarian, you would restrict your search to materials located in your own collection. Now you must make long-distance phone calls (unthinkable in most libraries) and spend a lot of time out of the library visiting sites. You will also learn how long it takes to do a job and how many hours are billable, that is, how many hours you could charge a client and how many hours are lost to unbillable time.

Meanwhile, while you are out visiting libraries and interviewing experts, what is happening to the rest of your life? By now your family members may realize you are pursuing a serious project similar to going to school or working a second job. They may understand that the next 6 to 12 months will prepare you for a lifelong profession that will pay off financially as well as emotionally. They may realize that this is a short period of time compared with retraining time in other fields. Accordingly, they will do everything they can to support you and make life easier so you can pursue your goals. Well, perhaps. More likely, you will receive little or no support from others. Your family may feel neglected and work at making you feel guilty in an effort to get you to stop. It may help you to know that this is a universal problem facing most women (and some men) who want to open their own businesses. (For advice on how to turn your family around, read *The Entrepreneurial Woman* by Sandra Winston, published by Bantam Books, 1980.)

Librarians may also try to talk you out of going on your own. They will bring up things like pension, paid vacation, insurance. But, if you are serious about this venture, do not listen. Tell yourself that they are too scared (or too sane) to leave their libraries, and promise yourself that you will come back and visit them a few years from now. By that time you will probably make double the salary they earn, work fewer hours, and have more peace of mind.

Do not expect much support from your friends either. They may listen politely the first time you talk about your plans, but do not expect them to sit through a progress report each time you meet. Resist the temptation to answer the question "What's new?" with a reply longer than a few words, or expect to lose your audience long before you finish your story on how you have just discovered a fascinating special collection at Upstate University.

And do not be discouraged by questions like "Still at it?" or "What kind of business did you say you were going to open?" or "You mean you expect people to pay you for that?"

Part of the problem of opening any business is developing enough confidence in yourself and your product to feel that you will be successful. When your product is *you*, it's especially difficult to feel confident.

Knowing that most people who want to start fee-based information services face the same problems you face may help you to realize that the lack of support is not directed at you personally. That is why it is so important to rely on yourself now and later. Listen to the experts, yes, but learn to trust your own instincts.

TAKING STOCK

Your fee-based information service will offer clients a top-flight product—your skills. Your ability to gather and organize information will pay your rent, buy your food, and keep you clothed. How much money you earn will depend on what services you offer and how hard you promote them.

Before you can sell your product—you—take stock. What are your skills? Pick up a pencil and a legal pad, and take an inventory.

Imagine a conversation between yourself and a clerk you have just hired to take inventory.

CLERK: What skills will you offer clients?

YOU: I'm a cataloger. I'll offer cataloging.

CLERK: That's it? Just one skill?

YOU: Yes, that's all I do. I'm a cataloger in a large university library. Work is departmentalized and I seldom do other work. My specialty is original cataloging of art materials.

CLERK: Doesn't sound like much, just one skill. Could you describe just what cataloging is?

YOU: Sure. Just this morning I cataloged a portfolio of oversized prints that arrived from a museum in Frankfurt. I began translating from the slip jacket.

CLERK: You mean you read German?

YOU: Yes, and French and some Spanish. (The clerk begins scribbling on the legal pad, but you continue.) I was very concerned about this particular portfolio because I had written a review of a similar portfolio for *Library Journal* and—

CLERK: So, you're also a writer and reviewer?

YOU: Well, I guess so.

CLERK: Tell me. Do you know anything about the value of art books? If a person wanted to know how much a bunch of art books is worth, could you quote a price?

YOU: Yes, I suppose I could appraise a collection.

CLERK (writing something on pad): Supposing I wanted to know which books to buy, could you tell me?

YOU: Yes, if you wanted me to recommend acquisitions or cite weaknesses in a collection, I could. (The clerk continues writing; you're getting a little annoyed at this point.) But I'd like to tell you more about my job as a cataloger for Upstate University. You see the classification system I designed for the special collection—

CLERK: The system you designed? I thought you said all you do is catalog books? Hang on a minute, I'm going to need more paper. This is going to be a long inventory of skills.

Keep your imaginary clerk with you as you examine your previous employment. What did you do before you started your present or latest job? Inventory all jobs even if they seem similar. By examining each separately, you can uncover subtle differences and add to your list of job skills.

Now, if you are a librarian, take a mental look at the courses you took in graduate school. The ordinary past has a way of fading, so if you cannot remember more than one or two courses, request a copy of your school transcript or examine the school catalog. (If you are not a librarian, try to think of courses you took that might be of help in this area.)

Why bother including this information on your inventory if you cannot even remember the name of a course? Because, although the content may have been forgotten, the skills are still inside your head and need only to be brought out and brushed up. If you do not remember courses, you cannot brush up. Skills learned in a long-forgotten course in children's literature could come in handy if you have to appraise a collection of children's books or organize a school library.

What library and information skills have you learned through your membership in library organizations? Think about those workshops you attended in previous years. Even if you were not able to apply the information to your jobs, you may be able to use what you learned when you start your new business. Did you compile a directory of members or serve on a committee to draw up a charter? Write it down!

By now you should have a list of skills that may surprise you by its length. It looks impressive—you never knew you knew so much! You have gone through every job you have ever had (including part-time jobs held as a student), remembered every course and every professor in your library or other professional school, recalled every workshop, seminar, or meeting of every organization you have ever belonged to. You have written down every skill you possess, from managing a large staff to running a photocopy machine. If you can run a photocopy machine and you did not write that down, your inventory is not thorough. Photocopying is a salable skill, and at times it can be very lucrative.

Up to now, we have been talking about library and information skills. But business skills are equally important. The world's greatest librarian could not succeed in a fee-based information service without business skills.

Fortunately, the ability to run a successful business is not inborn; it can be learned, and, in fact, it must be learned. People who have a flair for success in business may have learned to succeed either through formal education or by previously running businesses that were not successful. Ask the owner of your favorite restaurant if he or she has ever owned another business, and the answer may well be "Yes, several." Assuming business owners merely have a knack for success is similar to assuming that librarians merely have a knack for finding information.

An aggressive, extroverted personality is not required to run a successful business—even an information business. All types of people can succeed in business as long as they can identify their weaknesses and work around them. For example, two private catalogers who prefer not to see clients in person accept requests only by mail. Of course, they realize that limiting themselves means working even harder in this one area, so they have worked at developing a mailing list large enough to keep their business going.

Strengthening your weaknesses by forming a partnership with someone who is strong where you are weak is not usually a good idea. In theory it cannot fail; in practice it usually does. Most fee-based information services are not partnerships, but are owned by an individual who hires the employees. Some services that were formed as partnerships have dissolved, with the partners splitting to open their own companies.

Besides, you may not have all the weaknesses you think you have. Sometimes it is easy to think you cannot do something just because you have not enjoyed it or because you find it difficult. Let us take as an example a cataloger whose only contact with the public is the half hour she spends at the reference desk while the reference librarian has dinner. She really enjoys cataloging, but she hates that half hour as a relief reference librarian. She would like to start a freelance cataloging service, but she fears she would never be able to handle working with clients.

There are many reasons she might hate that half hour at the reference desk, none of which has anything to do with her ability to deal with the public. She may not have received adequate training, and this may make her feel incompetent and defensive. Perhaps she is so busy trying to do her regular cataloging assignments that she sees each reference question as an interruption that takes time away from important work. Maybe she is just hungry and resents waiting for the reference librarian to return so she can have her own dinner.

Think about what you consider your weaknesses and try to figure out the reasons behind them. Reexamining those areas may help you to discover new strengths.

CLIENTS

Now that you know what your product is—you and your skills—it is time to determine whether there is a market for your product. If so, is it large enough to support your business? The answer lies in the results of the market study you should undertake in your community.

First, you need to define "community." Think in terms of developing a sales territory. How large an area can you handle comfortably? How far do you wish to travel? Do not let "arbitrary" boundaries like city limits or state lines get in your way as you develop a territory.

Many businesses that fled high crime rates and inflated rents in America's large cities relocated in the shopping plazas of nearby suburbs. So, do not write off pastoral-sounding communities with names like Fresh Meadow or Countryside Hills; these suburbs could house the corporate headquarters of your biggest accounts. To get an idea of what companies are located in nearby suburbs, comb the Yellow Pages of area telephone books for manufacturers, corporate headquarters, and others.

The location of some fee-based information services allows their definition of community to include more than one state. Info/motion, in Lenox, Massachusetts, maintains as clients government agencies across the state line in Albany, New York. One California consultant who does little business in her own town insists that clients do not value a consultant's advice unless he or she has arrived via airplane to render it!

Large corporations are the biggest users of fee-based information services, but it would be foolish to limit your market study to this one area. Besides the business sector, you should concentrate on finding clients in education, government, associations, social agencies, and professions.

A community of any size will offer clients in all of these areas, although the numbers will vary. A large community does not necessarily offer more of all of these areas. For example, a fee-based information service in San Francisco can expect to find clients among its many colleges and universities, branch offices of national corporations, and a generally well-educated populace. It will, however, have fewer clients in government than a fee-based information service located in the California state capital of Sacramento, and probably fewer clients in social agencies and associations than a service in Los Angeles.

With the aid of several inexpensive maps, which you will need later when you begin to call on prospective clients in their offices, and Yellow Pages for every town you include in your "sales territory," you can begin to get a feel for your community. Check through the various Yellow Pages subject headings to get an idea of the types of businesses operating in your area. Look in the white pages as well for government agencies.

As you begin to identify specific clients, you should start a client file. A card file large enough to hold several thousand 3-×-5-inch index cards should see you through the first few years of business. On each card write the company name (or government agency, association name, and the like), address, phone number, type of business (if not obvious from the company name), and the name and job title of the individual to be contacted.

Never address a mailing piece to a job title and never make a phone call without first determining the name of the person you wish to speak to. You can find out individual names by calling the company and asking for the name of the vice president, librarian, or whatever, then calling back later and asking to speak to that person. Keep the file up-to-date so that you do not make the faux pas of asking to speak to someone who left six months ago.

Do not let this task of creating a client file become an exercise in recopying the telephone book. A company is not a potential client unless it needs your services. As you identify clients, think of which services you will offer to them.

Suppose you find the name of a company that manufactures solar energy heaters; which services could you offer? Theoretically, it could use many of your services; in practice, you could consider offering current awareness in the field of solar energy; you could reorganize its library or information collection, create one if necessary, start and edit a newsletter on solar energy to distribute to its clients, investigate how it can better market solar heaters, and so on.

Local newspapers will be a source of many clients now and in the future. Watch for announcements of new business openings, as well as expansion of existing businesses. Read news articles with the word *client* in the back of your mind. What services can you offer a new branch of a national business locating in your area? Will it need its own library now that it is physically removed from national headquarters?

An item on a school closing due to decreased enrollment should make you wonder how you can turn this bit of information into a job. Has the school board made its decision with the best available data, or have they used inadequate or outdated information? Can you save the town a costly error by doing a study? If the information is accurate and the school closes, what will become of the school? Can you put the school board in touch with a buyer for the building and its supplies? What will happen to the personnel that will be excessed? Can you write their résumés and research potential employers?

Your daily scan of newspapers should include general-interest papers, business journals, feminist newspapers, law reporters, and shoppers published in your area.

Soon you will see potential clients everywhere. At parties you will size up the guests in terms of their potential as clients. Your butcher, your hairdresser, your doctor, everyone is a client, and no one is safe from the mad client collector! This is as it should be because most everyone *is* a potential client.

One word of caution, however—do not steal clients from your soon-to-be former employer. Promoting your own business during working hours is unethical and could get you fired before you are ready to leave. You will also want to keep on good terms with your former employer because you do not want your reputation damaged. Besides, this employer is a potential client, too.

Can you identify enough clients? Enough means 2 to 5 percent of your market. If you feel that you need 5 major clients to keep your business going, you should contact a minimum of 100 to 250 clients.

MONEY

How much money you need before you can open your business is determined by your financial circumstances and the amount you choose to spend on setting up the service. Only you can decide how much money that is because you are the person in control of your financial situation. You are also the person who has to raise money if you do not already have it.

How much money you will need to live on is not necessarily the same as the salary you now receive. To get a more accurate idea of what you really earn, examine what it costs you to go to work each day and earn your salary. The cost of going to work includes transportation, lunch, clothes, union and/or other dues, charitable contributions made at work, pension fund deductions, and so forth. On the other hand, the cost of losing that job includes losing insurance benefits, tuition assistance, paid vacations, plus those little things librarians take for granted, like reading periodicals without subscribing and access to reference books.

If you are now paying off a large credit card balance or nearing the end of the endless job of paying off a car loan, your monthly expenses will be reduced in the future. If you can do it, you would be wise to pay off any debts before starting your new business.

What you cannot eliminate are your fixed costs: shelter, food, clothing, recreation. Although you cannot eliminate these expenses, if it means the difference between starting your business or not, you can do your best to make changes. Sharing an apartment is not unheard of, buying in bulk is nothing to be ashamed of, and who cares if your clothes are purchased out of season?

Nobody is suggesting that you live a subsistence life-style, but it is worth pointing out that when you receive a fixed salary, it is easy to allow your living expenses to match that salary. Once you take a look at where cuts can be made, you will see what is meant.

How much money should you spend on setting up your business? Again, it is up to you. The basics for any service business include letterhead, business cards, brochure, telephone, answering service or machine, and office equipment that can be purchased or leased. The amount of money spent on these items has little to do with your chances of success. Fee-based information services have been set up with capital funds ranging from zero[2] to upwards of several thousand dollars.[3]

Beyond the amount of money you spend setting up your business, you should think about a financial cushion. You cannot expect to live off your business from the very beginning unless you are able to attract enough paying clients before you begin, and even then you will encounter delays in getting paid by them. Once you begin, you will often run into frustrating periods either just after you have sent bills out or while you are working on a long-term project when you wait for large sums of money to reach you.

How large a financial cushion should be put aside? You can listen to the experts who say you should have between six months' and two years' income tucked away before you open a business, or you can develop alternative methods in case you do hit a slow period.

Could you obtain a short-term loan from a friend? Could you temporarily borrow against a life insurance policy? What about borrowing from a bank? One of the ironies of opening a fee-based information service is that the amount of front money needed is so small that traditional lending institutions, including banks and the

Small Business Administration (SBA), are not generally interested. Do go to SBA for expert advice, but do not expect a loan. Go to a bank for financial information, but do not expect a loan. Of course, both banks and SBA will allow you to fill out an application (they cannot refuse), but before you go through the frustration of applying for a loan, ask the officer how many similar loans have been made in the past year. The answer may surprise you.

So, where can you find start-up capital? Inventive Annette Hirsch saved $2,000 of her lunch money to open Information Specialists.[4]

What about a credit union? For women, many feminist credit unions sympathetic to women business owners have sprung up around the country. They cannot make loans to businesses, but they can grant personal loans up to several thousand dollars.

Relatives? If you borrow from relatives, beware of the trade-offs. For the privilege of no interest, you may have to put up with an overzealous interest in the inner workings of your business.

Spouse? Borrowing from a spouse presents a special set of problems. Will your spouse take your business seriously for long if you are not earning money? Will you be expected to pay back the loan in other ways, such as increased household duties? What happens if you get a divorce?

NEW GRADUATES AND RETIREES

For every handicap the new graduate brings to the operation of a fee-based information service, he or she brings a special strength. New graduates do not have years of job experience, but they do have a fresh education that includes study of the latest developments in the field. They have not yet built up a reputation in the library community, but they have access to the resources of the graduate school, including professors willing to recommend them for projects and fellow graduates who will need their services in a few years.

Retirees bring to the operation a lifetime of practical experience in the library world. Their education may have taken place a long time ago, but, no matter, they have the time now to update skills and learn new ones through continuing education. Their contacts in the field are many, so they will have little problem finding clients. A small but steady income from a pension relieves financial pressures.

STARTING A SERVICE IN YOUR CURRENT EMPLOYMENT

Perhaps you see the need for a fee-based information service within the public, corporate, or university library in which you now work, or perhaps entrepreneurship does not appeal to you and you would like to investigate the possibility of working in a fee-based information service within your current place of employment.

How can you go about starting a fee-based information service for someone else?

Whether you start such a service on your own or within a company or institution, the basics still apply. You must determine skills of personnel, sufficient market, potential for profit, and financial resources. Approach your supervisors after, not before, you have completed a market study. Simply suggesting the idea of a fee-based information service without proving its feasibility is not enough.

Beyond the basics, a few tricks of the trade from people who have started fee-based information services within companies may help you. Melinda Scott, senior consultant and director of Management Research Group at Peat, Marwick, Mitchell and Co., suggests first tapping the company's main pipeline by offering to sit in on meetings and getting involved in company planning. If you meet resistance to the idea of a librarian's sitting in at "important" meetings, research the meeting's agenda and put together and make available to the group a useful information package on topics to be discussed. Get the word out about your library's capabilities through company publications such as a newsletter or annual report. Start your own newsletter if necessary. Tell the company what your people can do and what they have been doing. An innovative friend of Scott's put together on her own the first national company information conference for her firm, in which she explained to executives from all over the company how information impacted on the company and what her staff was doing about it. The vehicle she chose to present information about her library, "the first national company information conference," sounded important enough for executives to feel obligated to attend.[5]

Connie Steward, manager of Information Services, General Electric, started with the same job title, but with the duties of a librarian. She now operates a fee-based information service that she created. Her advice to potential operators of fee-based information services within corporations is to become involved with every in-house training course because training is not complete without training in information-gathering techniques. For example, to engineers taking a short course in their field, Steward teaches a one-day segment on on-line searching of engineering data bases.

Connie Steward also believes in blowing her horn, something librarians are unaccustomed to doing. Brochures describing her fee-based information service are sent to internal clients on a regular basis.[6]

BASIC QUESTIONS AND ANSWERS

Q. What are some of the first things you must do when considering starting a fee-based information service?

A. Become familiar with all information resources in your area, learn the names of library personnel, start a resource file on information collections, make contact with special libraries.

Q. What skills are important in helping you to become an information broker?

A. Any library and/or information skill you learn in college, other courses, or on the job.

Q. Is it a good idea to form a partnership business?

A. In practice it doesn't seem to work in the fee-based information service area. Most services are owned by an individual who hires employees.

Q. How do you go about finding clients?

A. Undertake a market study of your community.

Q. Who are the biggest clients for fee-based information services?

A. Large corporations.

Q. What are some other sources of clients?

A. Education, government, and professional fields, as well as associations and social agencies.

Q. What are the basic money requirements for setting up a business?

A. Basic expenses include letterhead, business cards, brochures, telephone answering service or machine, and office equipment, purchased or leased.

Q. Can you get a loan from the Small Business Administration to start a service?

A. No, you can get expert advice from SBA, but no loan.

NOTES

1. "Profile," *Journal of Fee-Based Information Services* 2, no. 1 (January/February 1980): 9.

2. "Information Brokers: Who, What, Why, How," *Bulletin of the American Society for Information Science* 2, no. 7 (February 1976): 18.

3. "Information for Fee and Information for Free: The Information Broker and the Public Librarian," *Public Library Quarterly* 1, no. 1 (Spring 1979): 9.

4. "Information Brokers: Who, What, Why, How," p. 18.

5. Author's conversations with Melinda Scott, senior consultant, Peat, Marwick, Mitchell and Co.

6. Author's conversations with Connie Steward, manager, Information Services, General Electric.

GETTING
STARTED

What started out as a good idea has, after several months of your hard work, developed into a well-organized plan. Now it is time to put that plan into action. At last—it is time to get started!

HIRING CONSULTANTS

In the beginning, you may be tempted to handle all aspects of your business by yourself, from dealing with legal problems, to filing tax returns, to emptying the trash. Whether it is due to training for some women as a supermom that leads them to run their businesses one-person style, or lack of awareness of a better way, it is a common problem, especially among women business owners (although some men also fall into this category) to try to do it all themselves.

There are many reasons why you should not try to run your business entirely by yourself. The duties of running a business may leave you with little time each day to actually do your business. Filling out tax forms when you should be calling on prospective clients is no way to spend your working hours. Doing taxes in the late evenings or on holidays will only make you tired and less able to function well the next day.

Lack of sufficient knowledge needed to run a business makes for costly on-the-job training that can put a growing concern deep in the red, especially if your initial capital is limited. You cannot afford to learn your strengths and weaknesses by trial and error.

29

Alice Sizer Warner cautions that anyone who feels that hiring a lawyer or an accountant is a luxury cannot afford the luxury of starting a fee-based information service.

But professionals are expensive, you say! Yes, they are, but you do not need to hire a high-priced attorney like F. Lee Bailey or Melvin Belli, nor would you want to; they are simply not right for your purposes. You need a professional who is genuinely interested in helping a small business.

Do not hire a relative (this includes a spouse) and, worse yet, do not hire somebody else's relative. Get recommendations from other self-employed people and other small business owners. Find out who in town handles legal and financial matters for doctors, writers, carpenters, and the like.

Besides professional qualifications, you should take into consideration whether you feel you can work comfortably with the person you intend to hire. Do you feel intimidated? Are you interrupted often? Do you feel you are being patronized?

You need to find someone who takes you and your business seriously and who will give you the attention you deserve. After all, you are paying for it.

Establishing a relationship with an accountant or a lawyer in the early stages is preferable to waiting until a crisis develops. Armed with knowledge of your business, an accountant or lawyer is better equipped to handle problems as they occur. Without foreknowledge, dealing with a problem becomes a slow process because information must be gathered before action can be taken to solve the problem. And, remember, time is money.

What can you expect a lawyer or accountant to do for you and your business?

Your lawyer will help you determine the legal structure of your business, assist you in applying for necessary licenses, explain government regulations that affect your business, and generally keep you operating within the law.

Say goodbye to the short form forever! As a small business owner, you have entered the world of long forms—very long forms. Your accountant will help you fill out quarterly tax forms, estimated tax forms, and year-end tax forms. He or she will let you know when you are or are not making money, will establish a break-even point, and will identify tax deductions and devise an accounting system that suits you.

If you absolutely cannot afford a lawyer or accountant, and spending a few hundred dollars means the difference between starting with what you have or never starting, make use of free services. For instance, many feminist groups sympathetic to women business owners provide free legal and business services to women starting their own businesses. It is not uncommon these days for employers to provide legal insurance along with medical and dental insurance. Take advantage of this fringe benefit, if available, while you are still at your present job.

SETTING UP YOUR OFFICE

Where will you set up your office? In the World Trade Center? In the John Hancock Building? Fee-based information services are located in these and other prestigious office buildings around the country, as well as in not so prestigious buildings where the rents are lower.

But setting up an office does not necessarily mean that you must rent an office. Most fee-based information services are located in home offices either by design or by necessity. Sandra Ferguson, who owns Legwork Writers' Research Services, a company that provides research to motion picture and television writers and producers, finds working from her apartment, where she can receive calls at odd hours, preferable to sitting in a downtown office until the wee small hours of the morning waiting for calls from movie people, who are notorious insomniacs.[1]

On the other hand, Kathryn E. Taylor feels that a downtown office is essential for her type of business. Her firm, Taylor & Associates, specializes in library consulting services to the legal profession. Many of her law firm clients are located near her office in San Francisco's financial district. Although most clients never visit her office, her downtown location enables her to reach their offices easily.[2]

Some very successful fee-based information services began in home offices and relocated to office buildings when they outgrew their surroundings. Matthew Lesko ran Washington Researchers (Washington, D.C.) from his bedroom for the first six months of operation and moved to a suite of offices near the White House when he hired 35 employees.

Although some people attach a stigma to working at home —images of bootstrap operations, envelope stuffing, piecemeal sewing, and the like are conjured up in some minds —others recognize that historically professionals such as dentists, doctors, lawyers, accountants, and consultants, who could well afford to rent expensive offices, have chosen instead to work at home.

Operating a fee-based information service from the owner/operator's home makes sense for several reasons. The economic reasons include saving rent money throughout the year and taking an office-in-the-home tax deduction at the end of the year. Convenience is another factor. Rolling out of bed at 8:55, dressing casually, and never leaving important papers miles away at the office are fringe benefits not available to people who work in offices.

Operating a fee-based information service at home also eliminates the double commuting common to this business. Why commute to an office each morning only to have to commute again to a client's office or to an information source, then back again to an office to pick up messages, and again from the office back home each evening?

Working at home is not without its problems, however, especially when families are involved and particularly for women with families. Family members have traditionally not regarded mother's work in the same way they regard father's work, so the family may have to be trained to view mother's work as important even though she does not go to an office. Part of this training includes making the work area off limits whether or not the area is occupied; teaching family members not to interrupt during business hours except for an absolute emergency; and telling them not to expect errands to be run during working hours.

Besides teaching family members to respect their work, women who run fee-based information services from their homes must learn to respect themselves and their work. Cleaning the oven instead of calling on clients is no way to win respect from oneself. Trying to be a supermom who works her business around the needs of other people, gets all of the housework done by noon, chauffeurs the kids to tap dancing lessons at 3:00, and prepares dinner for her husband's clients at 6:00 can only lead to an early grave and the sabotage of her own business.

Getting down to business and resisting temptations offered by working at home are difficult even if the only temptation available is to knock off work early to wash windows, an activity that is, on some days, more appealing than balancing the company checkbook or making cold calls to prospective clients.

But whether or not a family is involved, working at home offers many temptations to those men and women who lack an absolutely iron will—which probably includes most of us. There is the garden. The television. The telephone. The refrigerator.

Setting up your office properly can help to eliminate some of the temptations. If you have a spare room that can be turned into an office, you have half the battle licked. The minute you close the door to your office, you have closed the door on numerous temptations, including the doorbell.

If you do not have an extra room, you will have to be especially clever about arranging your office. Les Nessman, news director of television's fictitious WKRP (Cincinnati) radio station, solved his "no office" problem by laying masking tape boundaries on the floor around his desk and ignoring visitors who refused to acknowledge his make-believe walls and door. And in *Worksteads*, a book by Jeremy Joan Hewes, architect John Edwards gives plans for a "bunker-style office" that creates a room within a room by rearranging furniture.[3]

Farfetched as Nessman's solution may seem, and whether you choose to follow Edwards's ideas, you do need to create a separate space for your office, both to satisfy the IRS requirement that space be used exclusively for business purposes to qualify for a home-office tax deduction and for your own comfort. Dual-purpose space will only eat up your time. You will not want to spend part of each morning converting your family or living room into an office and part of each evening converting your office back into a family or living room.

Basically, you will need only a few pieces of equipment for your office: desk, chair, bookcases, and a file cabinet to house clients' files and vertical file material. You will also need a telephone, answering machine or answering service, typewriter or occasional outside clerical help, access to a photocopy machine and data bases, and a tape recorder to record calls to experts.

As we have mentioned earlier, how much money you spend outfitting your office is entirely up to you. You need not worry about creating an impression for the benefit of clients—they will in all probability never see your office. You do, however, owe it to yourself to buy the best equipment you can afford. This does not mean the most expensive; it means what is best for you. If working at an old Dickensian desk, donated by a favorite uncle from his dry goods store, lifts your spirits and makes you feel good, use it. If this donation only depresses you because you long for glass and chrome, do not use it.

Shop around for office furniture; the prices vary widely. Besides stores that specialize in office furniture and office furniture departments of larger stores, look in neighborhood shoppers for ads placed by businesses selling their fixtures.

Shop around for phone service, too. Your telephone will be one of your largest business expenses, so it pays to get the best service for your money. Traditional phone service is no longer your only option. Today, telecommunications companies offer a variety of services, often at rates lower than your local phone company. MCI's or International Telephone & Telegraph's lower long-distance rates and use of a toll-free number through Toll Free America are alternative services that may be available in your area.

RemoteCall Forwarding, a service of the Bell System, redirects calls from other towns to your phone. The out-of-town client dials a number found locally in the phone book. The call is then redirected through phone lines to your office, and you are charged for a long-distance call plus a monthly service charge. Although the combined long-distance rates and monthly charge seem high, this is one way of tapping the market for your product in a nearby city that you might have missed otherwise.

Because you will be out of the office while you do research, you will need some means of telephone coverage. Your choices are to purchase an answering machine or hire an answering service.

Answering machines, although inexpensive when compared with answering services—the cheapest machine costs the equivalent of two months' worth of answering service; the best about the same as one year's worth of service—are not necessarily the best solution. Widely used by many professionals, the answering machine is still intimidating to some people, including well-heeled business professionals who become tongue-tied when faced with a talking machine. Some people would rather hang up than leave a message, which leaves you to wonder whether it was your mother who called ("You know how I hate to talk to that machine, dear") or a prospective client. Answering machines also cut people off after 30 or 60 seconds, run out of tape, and swallow messages whole.

For between $25 and $50 per month, you can hire a real live human being to answer your phone, take your messages, and hold them for you until you call. Added up over the years, an answering service can cost quite a large sum of money. But weigh the sum against the cost of losing even one important job to a machine before you make your decision.

If you anticipate using experts as a method of gathering information, you will need a small tape recorder that you can take with you on in-person visits to an expert's office. And for about $2 you can purchase a jack with a suction cup to stick on your telephone receiver to record phone conversations with experts. A word of caution: Always get permission to record any conversation before you tape it.

You will need to hire other outside help in addition to an answering service. If you do not type well, a reliable secretarial service is important. More important than typing speed is dependability. Will the often small but important jobs you give a typist be returned to you on time and typed without errors? Or will they be put aside while the typist completes bigger jobs for other clients?

Copying machines are just about everywhere, and you should have no trouble finding a coin-operated machine near you. But do not wait until you need a copying machine to start looking for one. Copy quality varies from barely readable to better than the original, so be sure to test a machine before you make plans to use it on a regular basis.

Gaining access to computer data bases also takes some advance preparation. The survey of information resources you undertook in Chapter 2 should have revealed universities and special libraries with data bases. Now all you have to do is make arrangements with the staff. If you have turned up nothing in your area, you can subcontract your searches to another fee-based information broker. Check listings in the *Directory of Fee-Based Information Services* to see which services are equipped with computer terminals.

NAMING YOUR BUSINESS

What should you call your business?

You could simply use you own name. Martha Ammidon Powers, Jay T. Tebo, and Mary M. Nash all operate successful businesses under their own names. Using your name for the name of your company is an especially good idea if you have worked in the library field long enough to build a reputation. People you have dealt with in the past will recognize your company name and connect it with your past accomplishments.

Or use your name in combination with a company name if you prefer not to sound like a one-person firm. Norman Lathrop added a word and christened his index-design company Norman Lathrop Enterprises. Other examples of personal/company combinations include Savage Information Services, named for owner Gretchen S. Savage; Taylor & Associates, owned by Kathryn E. Taylor; and Warner-Eddison Associates, Inc., named by its founders, Alice Sizer Warner and Elizabeth Eddison. It is hard to tell from these names alone whether the companies are composed of individuals or a large staff.

Your name is probably already listed in the phone book, which means that your business is also if you choose to use your own name for the business name. However, if you are a married woman, and your phone is listed in your husband's name only, your clients will have a hard time reaching you. Do not expect a prospective client to plow through male names from Alan to Zachary to locate you. And what happens if you change your name because of divorce or marriage? Should you also change the name of your business? These are problems that potentially affect all women, but that must be solved individually.

Suppose you sell your business or leave a business partnership that bears your name? Will you be barred from using your own name in another business?

It is not a good idea to name your service after yourself if you have a name that is difficult to pronounce or has an unusual spelling. Modify your company name if you must as did Henry Bloch. The famous tax preparer changed the spelling of his name to Block for fear he would be referred to as Mr. Blotch of H & R Blotch.

Whether or not you have employees, you can use a descriptive company name. A majority of fee-based information services use such names, and a majority of fee-based information services are run by individuals. The only legal requirement in most states is that you file a fictitious name statement and that the name you choose is not the same as one used by another company. Your county clerk's office will advise you of the fee to file this form and whether local laws require you to publish a notice in a local newspaper announcing your company name.

If you use a descriptive name, you will have to pay for business telephone service to have the name of your company listed. Technically, anyone using a telephone for business purposes is required to pay for business service, but some business owners choose to pay the lower rate for a residential phone by keeping the listing under their own name rather than listing the business name. Running the risk of being found out by the phone company is one thing; running the risk of losing prospective clients, who are told by an operator "I'm sorry, I have no listing for that company," is another.

If you operate your business from your apartment, you may find that your landlord prohibits you from posting your business name on your mailbox. This can be remedied by renting a post office box and receiving company mail at the post office. It is not uncommon for a business to have a mailing address that is different from its street address, so do not worry about it.

A descriptive name should be a blend of creativity and practicality. You want a name that creates the image you wish to sell and that accurately describes what you do. You will also want a name with room for expansion. The Ace Custom Cataloging Company is fine if all you plan to offer is custom cataloging, but somewhere down the line you may decide to add research and consulting to your services; then the name is no longer appropriate to the services offered by the company. Similarly, Boston Research Service sounds good, but if the rising cost of heating oil sends you south to Atlanta, you will have to face having a name that is out of sync with its location or having to change it.

Many fee-based information services use the word *information* or *library* in their names. Of course, you will not want to use a name that is the same as or similar to another firm's name, so do not use any of the names on the following list. (A little imagination can result in a unique title for your own service.)

Fee-Based Information Services Using *Library* or *Information* in the Name

Acquire Information
Biological Information Service
Business Information International
Chemical Information Center
Congressional Information Service
Decision Information Services, Ltd.
Environment Information Center, Inc.
Focus on Information
Geoscience Information Service
Government Information Services
Information Access Corp.
Information Alternative
Information Associates
Information Connection
Information Consultants
Information Control
Information for Business
Information Futures
Information Handling Services
Information Intelligence, Inc.
Information Management Specialists
Information on Demand
Information Plus
Information Professionals
Information Resource Consultants
Information Resources
The Information Retriever
Information Services
Information Services and Research
Information Specialists
Information Store
Information Systems Consultants
Information Yield
Library & Information Consultant
Library Consultant Service

Library Development Consultants
Library Information Service
Library Information Services
Library Reports & Research Service
Northwest Information Enterprises
Solar Energy Information Services
Technical Library Service
World Trade Information Center
World Trade Library & Business Information
World Wide Information Services

CREATING YOUR IMAGE

Initial judgment of your business will often be made on the basis of your image on paper. Therefore, a well-designed graphic identity, or logo, is important. Your brochure, letterhead, business card, and business forms represent you, and they communicate to prospective clients who you are and what you do.

You can hire a graphic artist to create your graphic identity and produce a graphic package. Or, with a little help, you can create your own image and do most of the work yourself—even if you flunked finger painting and cannot draw a bath!

Graphic identity has less to do with artistic talent than with marketing ability. An effective graphic identity can be established with a few words and simple artwork carefully chosen to correctly convey an image. A company's image can be one of exclusivity, specialization, universality, or whatever else the firm wishes to convey to clients and competitors.

Think about your own image. How do you see your business? Is it open, friendly, or exclusive? Would you rather be known for your low rates or for your high quality?

Think about your competitors' images, too. You may have to find a new slant if your image coincides with the images they present.

To heighten your awareness of paper identities, start a clippings file of business literature that strikes you as effective. Finding business literature, both good and bad, should not be too difficult; most of us come into contact with more than we realize. Flyers announcing new businesses are plastered on utility poles, handed to us in the street, and left on car windshields. Junk mail

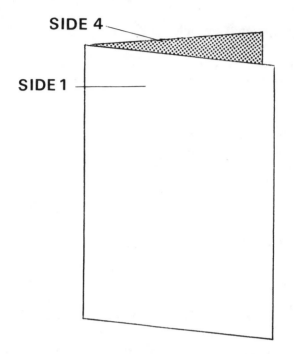

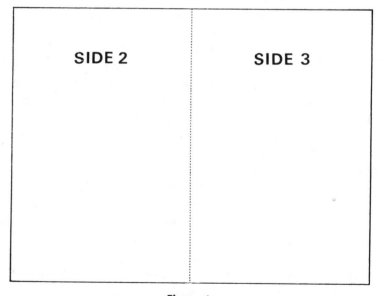

Figure 1

fills our mailboxes at home and at work. For a while, examine each piece you receive and determine why it is or is not effective. Do the graphic identity and text harmonize? Were you caught by what the piece says or how it says it? Did you fail to read a brochure because it looked impersonal?

Do the best job you can in creating your graphic identity because soon your carefully designed, painstakingly prepared mailing pieces will join the ranks of junk mail fighting to be read.

Remember that low cost does not necessarily mean low quality. If you have accurately pinpointed your market and carefully chosen an attractive graphic identity, you should have no trouble producing an inexpensive but effective package of business literature. A well-designed brochure is your most effective sales piece. The most popular format used by fee-based information services, as well as other types of businesses, is a 6½ by 8½ single-fold folder. This can easily be inserted into an ordinary business envelope and mailed as needed or mailed in bulk without envelopes.

To begin creating a dummy, cut a plain sheet of paper to size, fold it once, and mark the four sides, as shown in the dummy brochure in Figure 1.

Side 1, the front of your brochure, must catch the reader's eye and make the reader want to open the brochure and find out more. Side 1 should include your company name in easily readable letters in the upper half; your name and title, address, and phone number in smaller letters in the lower half; and your logo (if any) and slogan (if any). Keep side 1 simple, with plenty of blank space left all around.

Sides 2 and 3 comprise the inside of your brochure, its vital organs. Your job here is to convince the readers, your future clients, that your services are just what is needed to solve information problems they do not know they have.

Sound impossible? Not if you believe it yourself. Fee-based information services use a variety of methods to sell their services via brochures.

A long list of well-known clients will certainly make a favorable impression. But what if you do not have any former clients, well-known or obscure? Then use general categories of clients you hope to reach, for example, "We meet the needs of government agencies, national corporations, and small businesses." If you do use any actual names of clients, you must first receive permission to list them on your brochure.

Brief descriptions of several projects may convince a potential client to use your services. If you do not have a list of projects actually performed for clients, list projects you completed in previous jobs, for example, "Organized the information collection of a public library, designed computer software classification system used by a large university, searched data bases for a variety of clients."

Never merely list your services, however, without somewhere in the brochure explaining them more fully and connecting them to your prospective clients' information problems. The following list of services is fine, but it cannot stand on its own:

Acquisitions
Consulting
Cataloging
Abstracting
Indexing
Bibliography preparation
Thesaurus construction
Information systems design
On-line searching
Document delivery
Current awareness
SDI
Document retrieval
Technical services

These terms are not readily understood by people outside the information field, so you must explain each service in common language and how it will solve a client's problem; for example, to explain current awareness—"Do you have trouble keeping abreast of developments in your field? For only $25 per month our current awareness staff can provide you with tables of contents of journals in your field and supply you with photocopies of relevant articles."

An awareness that one profession's buzz words are another profession's gobbledygook will lead you to choose the right language for your brochure. Unless you number librarians among your clients, avoid using library lingo. In fact, some fee-based information services avoid the word *library* altogether and use euphemisms like *information collection*. In all cases, steer clear of weak words like *maybe, perhaps, should, could, help with*. Use strong, positive words and phrases. A quick look at the business section of any newspaper will reveal words like *dynamic, aggressive, determined,* and others. Words or phrases that spark interest from the business profession include:

Cost effective
Save (as in save money, save time)
Headaches (something you will cure)
Problem solving
Trouble shooting
Cost reduction
Professional
Technology
Information revolution
Information explosion
Impact
Decision maker
Profitable
Data
Information

Also, include any relevant information about your personnel, such as affiliations with organizations or special academic qualifications.

If you have a 24-hour answering service, provide discounts to nonprofit groups, or offer rush services, include this information as well.

Rather than quoting prices for each of your services, give a price range with mention of discounts or extra charges. Price quotes lock you into providing services at rates that cannot reflect the complexity of projects.

For *side 4,* turn the folder on its side so that the fold is on top. In the upper left-hand corner, place your return address. If you plan to bulk-mail the brochures, check with your local post office for current regulations and rates; then write your permit number in the upper right-hand corner; otherwise, leave this area free for a postage stamp.

To keep your mailing list accurate, include the phrase "address correction requested" in the lower right-hand corner. The post office charges a small fee for telling you when someone has moved, but in the long run it is less expensive to pay the fee than to lose even one client due to a wrong address.

You can take your dummy brochure to a graphic artist for completion or you can turn it into camera-ready copy for delivery to a printer yourself. Anyone who can draw a straight line with the aid of a ruler can learn to do layout by following instructions in any of several books on the subject, including *Print It* by Clifford Burke.[4] A few inexpensive materials (blue pencils, transfer letters, burnisher) can be purchased from an artists' supply store. Just tell the clerk what you plan to do and you may receive, along with the purchase of less than $10 worth of materials, a wealth of on-the-spot training in the art of producing camera-ready copy.

In general, there are few rules to follow. Neatness does count as the camera will photograph and reproduce anything it sees, including fingerprints and smudge marks. Less is better is a good rule when it comes to design. Do not try to cram everything onto sides 2 and 3 of your brochure. Leave lots of eye-pleasing space around your text. Break the text into artificially short paragraphs to give the reader a chance to absorb each sentence.

Your printer can help you straighten out any simple design problems. The printer can also help you choose the best paper at the most reasonable price. Until you have ordered paper, you do not know what confusion is. For starters, it is purchased by the pound, like cold cuts, not by the sheet. And although papers are available in hundreds of colors, some ordinary colors, like gray, are hard to find.

Once you have designed your brochure, designing your other business literature will be easy because you have done most of the work already.

Although not usually thought of as an advertising piece, your letterhead offers an opportunity to plug your services each time you mail a letter. Your letterhead should include your company name in easily readable letters across the top of the page; in smaller letters underneath the company name or at the very bottom of the page, place your address and phone number. In the upper left-hand corner, place your logo and slogan (if any) and your name and title.

Matching envelopes should bear your return address and logo (if any) in the upper left-hand corner. Include the phrase "return address requested" as on your brochure.

Press your letterhead into extra duty by making it serve as your invoice, purchase order, and other miscellaneous business forms. If you feel you have sufficient need for separate forms, design them to coordinate with your business literature.

For in-person calls in clients' offices and chance meetings with potential clients, you will need to have business cards printed. Business cards do little more than provide an introduction; they do not tell much about your business, and they are usually discarded, but they are customary in the business world and you will be asked for your card often.

Always exchange business cards whether or not you intend to use the other person's services. You will want to send a follow-up letter recalling how nice it was to meet—be sure to mention time, place, and date in case the other person has forgotten—and send along a brochure.

BASIC QUESTIONS AND ANSWERS

Q. When starting your own fee-based information service, who is the one professional you should not be without?

A. A lawyer or accountant; legal problems and taxes are not areas for do-it-yourselfers.

Q. Must you rent an office?

A. No. Although many information brokers do rent offices and some feel that a downtown location is essential, many run their businesses from their homes.

Q. What basic equipment is necessary to set up an office?

A. Telephone, answering machine or service, typewriter, tape recorders, and access to photocopy machine and data bases.

Q. What is the most effective sales item for an information broker?

A. A well-designed brochure.

NOTES

1. Author's conversations with Sandra Ferguson, Legwork Writers' Research Services.

2. "Profile," *Journal of Fee-Based Information Services* 1, no. 5 (September/October 1979): 5.

3. Jeremy Joan Hewes, *Worksteads: Living and Working in the Same Place* (New York: Doubleday, 1981), pp. 104–107.

4. Clifford Burke, *Print It: A Guide to Graphic Techniques for the Impecunious* (Berkeley, Calif.: Wingbow Press, 1972).

HOW TO
GET
CLIENTS

Once upon a time a man who lived in a large city in the eastern
United States decided to start a fee-based information service. He
quit his steady job and set up his service in a corner of his bedroom. Convinced that he could solve problems by providing the
best information and that others would want his service, he sat by
the phone and waited for customers to call.

Nobody called.

Something was wrong. He knew he could provide a valuable
information service that would give clients answers to unanswera-
ble questions. But he had no customers.

He decided to try out his service on a friend. He told the friend
to ask a question on any subject and he would provide an answer
within 24 hours—no matter what the question was or where he had
to go to get the answer. The friend asked a question about, of all
things, potatoes; should he invest in potato futures and why?

The man with the fee-based information service knew nothing
about potatoes, but within less than 24 hours he delivered more
information than his friend ever wanted to know about potato
futures.

Bolstered by this easy victory, the man was more determined
than ever to make his business succeed. So he continued to sit by
the phone waiting for customers to call.

Nobody called.

He sat by the phone for a total of six months and still nobody
called. Finally, as a last-ditch effort, he withdrew his savings and

printed 2,000 copies of a newsletter that described his fee-based information service and mailed it to local businesses and government agencies.

It worked. People called.

So many people called that within a few months he had to move his business out of his bedroom and into a large office downtown to accommodate his 35 employees. Today, he does nearly three-quarters of a million dollars in business each year.

If you do not think this is a true story, ask Matt Lesko, founder of Washington Researchers, Washington, D.C.

Despite the happy ending, this story is not meant to illustrate how you, too, can gross $750,000 per year. The moral of this story is: No matter how good your business is, or how badly its services are needed, no one will use it if he or she does not know about it.

METHODS OF BUILDING A CLIENTELE

Promoting your business is an activity that will occupy 20 to 25 percent of your time on a regular basis. During your first year of operation, you can expect to spend as much as 50 to 75 percent of your time building a clientele.

No business can succeed unless people know about it, but just letting people know about your business is not enough. Promoting a fee-based information service is more difficult than promoting a car wash, a bookkeeping service, a television repair service, a legal practice, or any other type of business that is readily understood by the general public. Before you deliver your sales pitch, you must know the individual problems of each of your prospective clients and how you can solve them. That is why the preliminary market research study you completed in Chapter 2 is vital.

Getting clients is difficult, but anyone who has accurately identified his or her market can sell his or her services with hard work. All types of personalities can succeed at selling. Gregarious behavior and a vicelike handshake usually associated with selling are not prerequisites for success. The key to successfully promoting a fee-based information service is to choose from an effective combination of methods to suit your personality.

Promotional activities include those that sell services directly to a prospective client on an individual basis, such as cold calls and direct mail, and less direct methods such as public speaking before groups. Let us take a detailed look at some of them.

Telling friends about your business. This is easy; it hardly seems like selling, but it is an effective means of promoting your business. In this no-pressure situation, you merely tell people you already know what you are doing these days, regardless of whether they ask you. Tell everyone about your new business—your doctor, your dentist, friends you have not seen in a while. Do not be a pest, but do follow up by sending a brochure. This evidence that you are serious (you have gone to the trouble of getting a brochure made) lends credibility to your business and reinforces what you have said.

Chance meetings. A supply of business cards and a patter about fee-based information services tailored to fit a variety of occupations prepare you to turn chance meetings into no-pressure sales meetings. The person sitting next to you on an airplane or standing in front of you in line at a bank could be your next client.

The subject of occupations comes up fairly early in conversations with strangers, so it should not be too hard to swing the talk around to fee-based information services. Tell the architect you meet at the butcher's how you can put his office in order with a new filing system for his blueprints. To a restaurant owner, illustrate what fee-based information services can do for her by mentioning selective dissemination of information on government regulations that affect restaurants.

Always follow up with a letter and brochure. Keep a name on your mailing list until you feel the cost of postage no longer warrants retaining it.

Joining organizations. There are two reasons why you should join a particular organization: because you are concerned with the goals of the organization and because potential clients belong. Martha Ammidon Powers, a Berkeley, California, freelance librarian, finds that many jobs come to her from other members of associations she belongs to.[1]

Nobody is telling you to join an organization whose goals clash with your own beliefs, but it is a good idea to join an organization you might not ordinarily belong to if it could be a source of clients.

Speaking to groups. Breakfast with the Chamber of Commerce, lunch with the Feminist Business Owners, dinner with the Tri-County Librarians' Caucus; speaking to organizations and associations increases your service's visibility in the community and introduces you to prospective clients in a professional atmosphere. As a featured speaker, you are presented as an authority on your subject who is treated with respect by the audience. Although your speech may be nothing more than a sales presentation, being asked to deliver it in front of a group, instead of fighting for a few minutes' time to deliver a sales pitch in an individual's office, places you in a power position.

Check calendars in the local press to see which groups invite speakers to their meetings. Contact an officer and explain why you think the group would be interested in hearing your speech. Once your offer is accepted, find out:

1. How long you are expected to speak.
2. Is a question-and-answer period customary?
3. Size of the expected audience.
4. Will you speak before, during, or after a meal?

A few days before your scheduled speech, call the officer to restate any requests for special equipment and to check on any last-minute developments.

"Be prepared" is the motto for the day of the meeting. If you are prepared, you can handle anything; anything from having your offer to answer questions greeted by total silence (not to worry —you have your own supply of "audience" questions written on index cards) to a case of nerves (of course, you've packed a talisman in your briefcase).

Speaking to a room full of strangers is not an activity that most people enjoy naturally. Women who are not accustomed to public speaking are at a special disadvantage because learned "feminine" mannerisms and inflections are sometimes interpreted by listeners as weaknesses. Yet, the ability to make an effective presentation of a business can be acquired, either through lessons with a speech coach or by reading books such as *Speaking Up,*[2] and should be acquired as a means of promoting a fee-based information service.

Press releases. Creating your own publicity by preparing a press release is an effective method of gaining attention from the local press. You will have a better chance of having your press release published if you use an unusual opening that sparks an editor's interest and if you follow accepted format to the letter, as shown in the sample press release in Figure 2.

In your opening paragraph, cite bizarre projects you have accomplished or pose unusual information questions that your service could answer if asked. In the paragraphs that follow, describe your business, starting with the most important aspects expanded with supporting points. So-called pyramid style (most important to least important) is used because editors cut a too-long release from the bottom up.

Send your press release to general circulation newspapers, business newsletters, feminist presses, and other appropriate media

---

(your letterhead)   NEWS RELEASE
                                                  For Immediate Release

NEW BUSINESS SAYS ASK US ANYTHING

Your town, state, today's date—How many fish swim in Lake Erie? Are waterbeds dangerous to your health? Do turtles cough?

"These questions are typical of the type we receive at The Information Service," says the company's owner, Martha Smith.

On an average day, The Information Service provides answers to between 20 and 30 questions posed by local business owners, government officials, and others who hire this service on a per-question basis.

All employees of The Information Service hold advanced degrees in information science and have worked in the field for a number of years

# # #

For more information contact: Martha Smith, 1234 Street, your town, zip code, telephone number (include area code).

Figure 2

in your area. After a week, call the editor of each periodical and offer to provide any further information about your business—this could lead to an offer to interview you for a feature article about your service.

Do not be disappointed if the editor does not know who you are or what you are talking about. Volunteer to send another press release, and place a follow-up call within a week after you send it.

Advertising. Ordinarily fee-based information services do not use paid ads as a method of promoting their businesses. There are exceptions: FIND/SVP has advertised in the business section of the *New York Times,* but not on a regular basis. London Researchers places ads in library publications in England, primarily to keep its name visible in the library community, not as a means of obtaining clients.

Placing small but regular ads in specialty newsletters is one form of low-cost advertising used by some fee-based information services to interest new clients from a particular field. Sandra Ferguson's ad for Legwork Writers' Research Services regularly appears in the *Writers' Guild of America West Newsletter,* a publication read by screenwriters. Mary Tomaselli places ads for her indexing services in such publishing journals as *Editor and Publisher* and *Publishers Weekly.*

Exhibits. The high cost of renting floor space at a national conference prohibits all but the largest fee-based information services from participating in conferences. However, if less expensive space can be rented at local conferences, an attractive booth exhibit can be an effective means of increasing visibility and attracting new clients.

Direct mail. Introducing your service by mail is an inexpensive means of reaching a targeted audience. It is good practice for new and established fee-based information services to keep their mailing lists active. Through direct mail, you can keep in touch with clients and also announce new areas of expertise or changes in personnel.

Initially, you will bulk-mail your brochure to a large list of potential clients and continue adding to your list each week. In its early stages of operation, Warner-Eddison Associates, Inc., set a goal of mailing eight brochures per week to names suggested by friends and culled from newspapers.[3]

For your mailing to be effective, your brochure must reach the right person. Addressing a mailing piece to "Marketing Department" or "Library" brands it junk mail. Do your homework and find out the name of the individual you want to reach.

Once you have introduced your services by mail, following up with a phone call to the person who received your brochure is a low-stress promotional situation. You are not selling anything; you just want to ask for a chance to drop by and explain how you can solve the company's information problems and save it some money. Who could refuse an offer like that? Lots of people will not.

Direct contact. Sitting in a stranger's office trying to sell your services is one of the most difficult, albeit effective, methods of reaching clients. A large percentage of business is obtained by fee-based information services through individual sales calls with clients. One major Canadian firm says direct contact accounts for 75 percent of its business.[4]

A well-prepared sales presentation can make the prospect less grueling. Barbara Felicetti of Info/motion says:

I always do a lot of research about a potential client before I make a call. I try to find out what their problems are, how I can help them, and point out what the consequences might be if they don't use information to make decisions.[5]

As soon as you arrive at a client's office, quickly establish yourself as someone with important business. Look the part of an important, confident person; that means well-tailored clothes and a high-quality attaché case (no one will know if it's your only suit, or that your briefcase holds nothing more important than your lunch). Hand your business card to the receptionist and introduce yourself as Ms. (or Mr. or Mrs.) So and So of Such and Such Company and ask to see Mary Smith, not Miss or Mrs. Smith, or Tom Smith, not Mr. Smith.

Business people are accustomed to salespeople's dropping by unannounced, and they will often see a person if only to make sure they are not missing something important.

If Tom or Mary Smith is free, he or she may see you for a few moments. If he or she is out or in a meeting, get an appointment for later in the week. If you are asked to wait, do not offer to wait more than a few minutes. Your time is as valuable as that of the person you want to see. And if you are convinced that Tom or Mary Smith is the person you should see, do not accept an offer to meet with an assistant. Push for an appointment with the main person.

Listings. Promote your business free of charge through listings in business and library publications. Locally you will find many opportunities to list your company in business directories, but steer clear of a guide that charges for an entry unless you have determined by calling other companies that the guide is produced by a bona fide publisher. There are some disreputable publishers who make money by charging high prices for listings and then distributing bogus business guides only to the companies listed.

Whenever possible, take out association memberships in the name of your business so that your listing in the annual membership directory will appear under your company's name.

National exposure is available free through annual listings in publications such as *Information Industry Market Place* (R. R. Bowker), *Consultants and Consulting Organizations Directory* and *Speakers and Lecturers: How to Find them* (Gale Research), and *Directory of Fee-Based Information Services* (Information Alternative). *American Libraries* charges a reasonable fee for space in its "Consultants Keyword Clearinghouse," a feature appearing in the magazine four times a year.

Referrals from other fee-based information services. Surprisingly, your competition can be a source of jobs. Informal working arrangements exist between services for a number of reasons. A freelance librarian working on a long-term job does not want to disappoint a client, so she might subcontract an indexing job to your company instead of turning it down. Your archenemy, a big literature-searching service downtown, has access to hundreds of data bases, and you go there when you have on-line requests. They might turn over a small consulting job to you the next time you visit.

Tina Byrne, of Regional Information and Communication Exchange at Rice University, says: "We have a warm and cordial working relationship with area information brokers and we refer clients to another broker or to whatever source is appropriate."[6]

Word of mouth. In a survey of fee-based information services undertaken by Information Alternative, word of mouth was given as the number one most effective method of obtaining clients.

Why not mention that fact straight away? For two reasons. First, as a new service you cannot expect word of mouth to work for you. You must build up your business before clients begin to talk about your work to others and recommend that they contact you. Second, there is not much you can do directly to secure word of mouth. People either tell others about your company or they do not. Clients either refer customers to you or they do not.

Indirectly, however, there is much you can do to encourage word of mouth. Getting the word out with ads, listings, press releases, speeches, and so on, makes you visible, and the more people there are who know about you and your work, the more people there are who will talk about you. In the area of client relationships, asking them to act as sales representatives is not advised. Just let your work speak for itself, and your clients will recommend you to others if the services you provide are first-rate.

DEALING WITH CLIENTS

Working successfully with clients requires learning a new behavior because when dealing with clients, you are neither employee nor boss. The position is at the same time one of power and one of impotence. As an outsider employed on a per-job basis, you are both expert and hired hand. You receive no fringe benefits or job security, yet your hourly fee may be triple that of your in-house counterpart.

Learning the rules of the game through observation and by talking to consultants and freelancers in other fields will help you to avoid errors that could cost you dearly.

Creating a powerful image through dress and attitude forces others to react in a positive way. Unfortunately, in our "instant" society, impressions are often formed too quickly, and how a person looks is one way of judging that person. This does not mean that to be successful you must follow a formula that requires investing in uncomfortable high-heeled shoes, pin-striped suits, or the latest in designer ties. Dressing tastefully, whatever you wear, is what communicates power.

A serious attitude toward your profession makes others see the value of your work. It will not be long before someone in your client's office says something like: "The boss could have saved a bundle by hiring a secretary for five bucks an hour to get this library in shape." Letting a remark like this pass or reacting with anger puts you in a defensive position.

What should you do? Practice preventive medicine. Unless you have been advised that the project is confidential, take the initiative at such a time to introduce yourself to others and explain how they will benefit from your work. Make certain that others in the company, besides the person who hired you, know who you are and why you are there.

Try to do much of your work away from the client's office, if possible. Working at home or in a library away from the site will free you from interruptions and idle time-wasters that are a part of the 40-hour work week. Taking a coffee break with the rest of the staff while you are being paid $50 an hour is a sure way to make the boss bring up the question, "Can we afford this?"

If you have to work in-house, be friendly to your co-workers, but do not blend in so much that you begin to contribute to office politics. It is as natural for friendships to form between yourself and others as it is to be treated with hostility by some. Employees may feel your presence is a threat to their employment, a signal that they have not done their jobs well.

Women have some special problems when dealing with male clients. Although no serious cases of harassment have been reported by owners/operators of fee-based information services or their staffs, subtle harassment goes on every day. A study undertaken by the University of California at Santa Barbara reports that men account for 96 percent of interruptions in conversations between men and women. The study also found that men change the subject more frequently than women and fail to follow up on topics introduced by women.[7] An awareness that this behavior is culturally learned, not personally directed, might help you to be more assertive when you deal with male clients.

KEEPING CLIENTS

Providing high-quality service at reasonable rates does not necessarily ensure that a client will return to you in the future. Obviously you cannot expect all clients to need your services again—

businesses fold, merge, and relocate. Some jobs are "one shot" in nature. Once you have researched a company for a job seeker and the person has been hired due to your efforts, there is no reason to provide the same service for that person again. The staff you selected to run a library you organized may work so well that your former client has no reason to call for your services again.

Encouraging clients whose business you can reasonably expect again is worth the extra time and effort. Information Specialists of Cleveland estimates that about one-third of its jobs are repeat business.[8]

On the job, keep your eye out for more work. Your client knows what a great job you are doing indexing this year's annual report; what about indexing the quarterly reports? Can you sell document delivery to a client who asked for a bibliography?

Shortly after you complete a job, make a follow-up call or visit suggesting new projects and determining the aftereffects of your work. You cannot expect future assignments if there is any question about the value of a previously completed project.

An odd phenomenon in the consulting business causes a report to stick fast to the desk of the person who ordered it, thereby preventing the findings of the report from being given to the rest of the staff. Although there is no scientific reason for this bizarre occurrence, there is an easy way to free a report from the grips of a rolltop desk. Offer to drop by and discuss the report or to provide (free of charge) an abstract. A well-written report should speak for itself, but sometimes a little reassurance that the report is not all bad news will get it off the desk and into the right hands.

Keep in touch with former clients through inexpensive promotional methods. Your annual Christmas card reminds a client that you are still in business and lets you know whether the client is.

Announce new services through printed flyers with an added personal note and send letters of congratulations when you hear of their accomplishments.

BASIC QUESTIONS AND ANSWERS

Q. How much time does the information broker spend on building a clientele?

A. During the first year, as much as 50 to 75 percent.

Q. What are some of the ways to build a clientele?

A. Tell your friends about your new business, turn chance meetings into no-pressure sales meetings, join organizations, speak to groups, send out press releases, and advertise.

Q. What are some other ways of introducing your service?

A. Exhibits at local conferences, direct mail, free listings in business and library publications, referrals from other fee-based information services.

NOTES

1. "Profile," *Journal of Fee-Based Information Services* 1, no. 2 (March/April 1979): 6.

2. Janet Stone and Jane Bachner, *Speaking Up* (New York: McGraw-Hill, 1977).

3. Alice Sizer Warner, "Information Services—New Use for an Old Product," *Wilson Library Bulletin* (February 1975): 443.

4. "Profile," *Journal of Fee-Based Information Services,* 2, no. 2 (March/April 1980): 9.

5. Ibid., 1, no. 1 (January/February 1979): 8.

6. Ibid., 2, no. 5 (September/October 1980): 9.

7. Carol Lynn Mithers, "When You Talk, Does He Listen, and If Not, Why Not?" *Mademoiselle* (March 1980): 199.

8. Information Specialists sales and promotional materials.

SERVICES
OFFERED BY
BROKERS

This chapter consists of an annotated list (in alphabetical order) of services that information brokers may offer.

Abstracting. Offered as one service to speakers and researchers needing background information, or in conjunction with the preparation of a bibliography, data base, or other large project, this basic but versatile skill commands $5–$25 per hour, with an average of $15.

Analyzing information. To analyze information, you must employ (or be) a subject specialist capable of writing a cogent report based on your research. As part of a year-long project on aging, Documentation Associates (DA) temporarily retained the services of a group of prominent gerontologists who examined information gathered by DA's staff. Together their work resulted in a 3,000-page report.

Ordinarily you will not be expected to analyze information; in fact, one service states in its brochure that it cannot analyze the information provided. If, however, you are called on to analyze information you have gathered and you hire a subject specialist, you should receive a finder's fee or a portion of the hourly rate to recoup your time spent locating and working with a specialist.

Your financial arrangements should not be made known to your client; that is, if you bill the client $50 per hour for services, the client should not be told that $40 per hour is for the subject specialist and $10 per hour is for you. Nor should the subject specialist know these arrangements.

Appraising collections. Do not librarians (and perhaps some other people) harbor a secret dream of rummaging through dusty volumes in search of that priceless first edition only *she* (or he) can recognize for its true value? Appraisers earn $25 per hour and up.

Bibliographies. Technically these are not bibliographies as defined by the library profession. Proper bibliographic form is disregarded or modified as appropriate to the user's needs. A variety of formats besides books must be listed in a bibliography to fill a request for "everything ever written on such and such" or "everything published in the last five years on such and such."

Fees for bibliography preparation run between $15 and $25 per hour plus expenses, such as on-line connection time.

Shrewd marketers sell related services as part of a bibliographic package—abstracts, document delivery, annotations, and others.

Cataloging. For clients who think cataloging is thumbing through the latest Sears wish book or Burpee spring seed catalog, terms like "organizing" and "arranging" are used. Anybody with information or things (butterflies, buttons, maps, musical instruments) is a candidate for cataloging services.

Depending on clients' needs, some fee-based information services act as consultants who recommend a system to be implemented by a client's in-house staff, in which case consultant rates of $25–$100 per hour are charged.

With contract cataloging, the actual process is undertaken by the fee-based information service staff at $5–$25 per hour, plus an initial consultation to determine the plan of attack.

After the job is complete, to accommodate new acquisitions received in the future, a client may choose to have a staff member trained in cataloging or may opt for regular maintenance visits from the fee-based information service.

Clipping service. Packaged Facts is perhaps the best known in this area. From a library of 5,000 magazine issues going back as far as the early 1930s, Packaged Facts retrieves clippings to help marketers measure the impact of a campaign, manufacturers keep track of competitors, and lawyers gather evidence.

A few smaller services without extensive in-house libraries have joined the back-dated clipping service, for which they charge $25–$50 per hour. Actual old clippings are not provided by any service. Photocopies cut to resemble clippings suffice.

Computer software design. Fees charged for creation of software vary depending on the job. Future Shack, Information Access Corporation, Cuadra Associates, Inc., and others specializing in computer software design have combined information-gathering skills and facilities with computers to develop new computer products. Software is designed for an individual client or published by a fee-based information service, then sold to subscribers.

Consulting. Clients pay between $20 and $100 per hour for advice from library or information consultants. An hourly rate of $100 may seem high compared with a librarian's salary, but use of a consultant results in savings if cost-effective solutions to information problems are found. For example, the consultant who devises a selection policy that avoids duplication in branch offices will save a national corporation thousands of dollars over the years.

The end product of a consultant's work is usually a report delivered verbally to the client or submitted in writing. Because the report does not solve the problems, but recommends solutions, the consultant may return wearing a different hat to carry through on a recommendation if appropriate.

For example, Minne R. Motz, a school library consultant, might evaluate the collection of an independent school seeking accreditation. Her duties as a consultant end with her report suggesting ways to fill gaps in certain areas to bring the library up to par. The school can either buy materials following her guidelines or use her services as an acquisitions librarian to close the gaps.

Current awareness. Fees charged for providing photocopies of journal tables of contents pages in a specific area often depend on the costs involved in obtaining the journals. To make it worthwhile, current awareness should be sold on a contract basis with the annual fee collected in advance. Document delivery can be tied in to a current awareness contract.

Directories. In addition to producing and distributing directories through their own companies, fee-based information services assist publishers in the preparation of directories and create in-house directories for organizations at $15–$25 per hour.

Displays and exhibits for libraries. A few fee-based information services specialize in the design of displays and exhibits. Joyce Firestine of Arizona develops summer reading program displays for which she charges $5 per hour; Jill Woolums charges $15–$25 per hour to design exhibits for business and law libraries.

Document delivery. Document delivery means providing copies of written information to clients. It sounds so simple! Your client wants a copy of an article, so you go to the local library, use the coin-operated photocopy machine, and send the copy off to the client.

If only it *were* that simple. Document delivery can either earn you a decent living or drive you crazy by eating away your profits. If the article, book, dissertation, government report, or whatever is not available at a local library (and it seldom is), you must locate it through another means—interlibrary loan or data-base producer—and deliver a copy to your client within 24 to 72 hours.

You may spend half a day searching for an article and earn $5 for your efforts. Charging for a searcher's actual time would make the cost of document delivery prohibitive so only direct costs plus a small profit margin are billed to clients.

Information Intelligence, Inc., charges $5 per item if it is available through its own sources and $8 if an outside source is used, plus, in all cases, copyright fees, postage, connect time, and so on, which are rebilled to clients.

Small doses of document delivery can be profitable if you tie it in with current awareness or some other service in which you have already located the document and need only make a photocopy to earn your $5.

At times it is less trouble to work through a fee-based information service that specializes in document delivery and charge your client a small amount above cost rather than trying to locate a single document. Companies such as Information Intelligence, Inc., and Information on Demand do well by working in volume, but a large-scale operation requires a substantial investment in electronic equipment.

Editing. For $5–$15 per hour, fee-based information services edit brochures, technical reports, financial reports, promotional materials, and other publications.

Editorial services. Universities, associations, hospitals, businesses, printers, and publishing houses need occasional editorial assistance. Over the past years the amount of work available to freelance editorial workers has increased as in-house staffs have shrunk. Enter the fee-based information service! You will not make a fortune as an editorial freelancer (fees range from $5 to $15 per hour with a few services billed a bit above that range), but if you are skilled, you will find plenty of small jobs to fill odd hours between larger, higher paying jobs.

Besides editing, fee-based information services offer indexing, typing, proofreading, book design, fact verification, abstracting, bibliographies, dust jacket copywriting, research, and picture research.

Evaluating information needs. Needs assessment is a superficial form of consulting. After touring the in-house library or information center and speaking with personnel, you prepare a brief report identifying areas of concern and deliver it to the client. The client is free to write you a check for your efforts and show you the door or to hire your firm to reorganize the collection, purchase new acquisitions, or whatever is needed to fill those information needs.

Grants. Fees for researching and writing grant proposals range from $15 to $35 per hour with discounts given to nonprofit organizations. Umbrella Associates of California, which specializes in preparation of grant proposals for artists and art organizations, charges $35 per hour for its services.

Identifying experts. "If you need information on the future demand for peanuts, there is an expert. . . . If you want details about the latest technology for nuclear waste disposal, there is an expert. . . . If you are interested in the prospects for the zinc industry, there is an expert. . . . If you need to keep track of the latest trends in mergers and acquisitions, there is an expert. . . . If you want to know how people spend their money, there is an expert."[1] So says Matt Lesko, the expert on finding experts. Lesko swears by using experts to solve information problems. In an interview in the *Journal of Fee-Based Information Services,* he explained why.

> Because much of our work deals with the problems of today, and tomorrow, we cannot rely upon information that already appears on a library shelf. Consequently, the largest portion of our information is derived through interviews with acknowledged experts and observers.[2]

Indexing. Joy of Indexing is what Robert Zolnerzak calls his freelance company. Although some of us may not share Zolnerzak's unbridled enthusiasm for indexing, it is a skill that brings in jobs both large and small. His projects include cookbooks, medical journals, religious periodicals, encyclopedias, and conference proceedings.

Freelance indexers also publish their own indexes. *Index to Model Making and Miniatures,* which covers 100 craft and hobby magazines, is published annually by Norman Lathrop of Ohio, for example.

Industry overview. Providing an overall picture of an industry or product involves research, interviewing experts, and report writing.

Fees are arranged on a per-project basis or at $10–$35 per hour.

Instant education. This service provides everything a client always wanted to know about something in a hurry. For example, shortly before boarding a plan for Washington, D.C., a client in California called Info Mart to say he was delivering a speech to the Department of Defense that afternoon on alternative uses for a computer manufactured by his own company. Did they know of any alternative uses for computers? By the time the client reached the airport, he had been provided with a minicourse to study during the cross-country flight.

Users of instant education include job seekers, speech writers, and consultants. Rates range from $15 to $25 per hour.

Literature searching. Manual searches are billed by the hour ($15–$35) with higher rates charged for searches that require special knowledge or that must be translated.

Loose-leaf updating. Loose-leaf binders are a familiar sight in law firms. So are stacks of loose pages that legal secretaries do not have time to file. Learning to maintain a loose-leaf product is not difficult, but as with any other skill knowledge of basic procedures and practice are necessary to work efficiently.

Knier Associates, a fee-based information service in Milwaukee that serves the needs of the legal community, publishes a training manual called *Filer's Guide.* The guide stresses the importance of hiring qualified personnel rather than expecting a secretary to squeeze filing in between typing and answering the phone. The guide also examines major loose-leaf services and their idiosyncrasies.

Normally, loose-leaf updating is sold on a contract basis with filers making weekly or biweekly visits to designated law firms. You should also consider offering emergency filing service at a higher hourly rate to accommodate clients with rush jobs.

Maintenance of collections. Keep up the good work! To prevent time and use from eroding a recently organized collection, sell maintenance as a follow-up service to provide for its upkeep. A librarian sent in on a regular basis to maintain a collection too small to need a full-time librarian can handle technical service, provide reference service, and recommend new acquisitions.

The most profitable method of selling maintenance is on a long-term contract basis. Overestimate the number of visits to accommodate for any projects introduced at a later date or to provide for complications. Once you are on the job it is easier to decrease the number of hours spent on maintenance than it is to ask for an increase.

When a collection is turned over completely to in-house staff after organization is completed, maintenance takes the form of training. Through a combination of custom-tailored procedures manuals and workshops, nonlibrarians are provided with basic knowledge of collection maintenance and given guidelines on procedures.

Market research and survey preparation. Market research questions posed to fee-based information services are fascinating, but no less so than the methods used to find the answers.

For example: What is the market for a collection of 4,000 tape measures I just inherited? What new market can I find for inexpensive cassette players manufactured by my firm? How many rental cars are available in the United States?

Warner-Eddison Associates, Inc., took the direct approach and put the person with the unlikely inheritance in touch with an auctioneer who sold the collection. While doing an on-line literature search on cassette players, Fred Bellomy of Info Mart noticed an article that mentioned that cassette players were often used by home computer owners to store programs. He supplied his client with a mailing list of home computer owners. Matt Lesko called the Department of Transportation and found an official with statistics on rental cars.

Market research also means writing lengthy reports such as those prepared by Packaged Facts. Its average custom-tailored market study runs 100–200 pages, takes a month to complete, and costs in the neighborhood of $2,000–$3,000.

Because it is often difficult beforehand to determine whether the answer will be found in a single phone call or take a month of digging, the client should be given an estimate and receive frequent progress reports if it appears that the research cannot be completed within the estimated price.

On-line searching. Unless you plan to purchase or lease a computer terminal, you will have to gain access to data bases through a local university or subcontract your on-line searches to a fee-based information service equipped to handle requests.

Computer data bases are not a cure-all, but you should become familiar with various commercially available files through directories published by users, sales literature from suppliers, and hands-on workshops sponsored by library schools and suppliers.

And knowing when not to do a search on-line is as important as knowing how to use a computerized data base. Fees for searches vary according to the amount of connect time needed to complete a search and the type of data base used.

Organizing collections. Every business, association, or group collects information, huge amounts of it. But few companies, associations, or groups know how to organize their information collections. Not only do fee-based information services know how to organize information, they know how to organize information so that time and money are saved.

Like other fee-based information services, Warner-Eddison Associates, Inc., has provided its clients with cost-effective solutions through organization. While organizing an engineering firm's library, they discovered engineers designing a product that made use of a part that (unbeknown to them) had been out of production for the last five years. The engineers had consulted a five-year-old parts catalog because they could not find the current catalog. Organization spared these engineers from creating a costly and worthless product.

To organize collections, you must have a good grasp of the basics of cataloging and classification and the cleverness to apply these basics to information in any form—architectural blueprints, catalogs, videotapes, maps, X rays, photographs, books, microforms, documents, and so on.

Before you begin, talk to the people who use the information as well as the executive who hired you. Informal conversations with users will uncover specific needs and determine the design of a practical retrieval system. Through training sessions and procedures manuals provided by you, in-house staff will be able to operate the collection on a day-to-day basis.

The service of organizing collections is sold on a contract basis with provisions made for maintenance visits. It is also sold on an hourly basis with consultants fees paid for hours spent determining needs and designing retrieval systems and clerical rates paid for the tasks of labeling, filing, shelving, and other routine chores.

Part-time librarians and temporary replacement of librarians. When a teacher is sick, a substitute is called in. When a doctor attends a conference for a few days, a standby is on call. When a secretary goes on vacation, a temporary office service may provide a replacement.

But when a librarian is sick, attends a conference, or goes on vacation, what does the library do? Usually nothing. Except for school librarians, libraries normally do not call in librarians from the outside to replace in-house staff on a temporary basis. Why? Tradition.

Tradition prevents libraries from hiring part-time librarians to handle overloads as businesses do. Tradition prevents libraries from hiring part-time librarians to replace librarians on leave. Tradition prevents libraries from hiring part-time librarians to deal with tasks that in-house staff never has enough time to do.

Wayne Gossage of Gossage-Regan Associates suspects that the tradition of lack of money forces academic libraries to use relatively inexpensive student labor and public libraries to go without rather than hire part-time librarians temporarily.

Selling part-time librarian services to businesses is easier than selling to academic and public libraries because businesses are accustomed to using outside personnel services. It is, of course, possible to take a long-term part-time job as a library's regular employee and run a part-time fee-based information service for short-term jobs.

Since 1974, Martha Ammidon Powers has made her living by working a variety of part-time library jobs and freelance projects. At one point she worked a few days a week at the Social Action Research Center in Berkeley, California, staffed a special night reference line at a public library in Berkeley, and pursued several short-term projects.

Personnel selection. Once you are in business, you will be contacted by librarians looking for work. Hold on to those résumés! You will need the name of a good librarian when you must find someone to fill a position you have created in a newly organized library.

If you function as a personnel consultant, you should charge a fee similar to that of an employment service, that is, either a flat rate or a percentage of the first year's salary.

Photo and picture research. To provide photo and picture research services, you must be located in New York, Los Angeles, Chicago, or another major city rich in photo and picture sources, or subcontract requests to a freelance photo and picture research service in one of these cities. Although it is possible to locate and request specific pictures at a distance, Rosemary Eakins of Research Reports, a fee-based information service specializing in the location of visual images, cautions that there is no substitute for lengthy in-person visits to picture suppliers. She asks: "Why limit yourself to published pictures when you can go to the source?"[3]

Picture Research (Washington, D.C.), After-Image (Los Angeles), Research Reports (New York), and other fee-based information services provide photo and picture research services to advertising agencies, book and periodical publishers, filmstrip houses, and television and motion picture producers.

Contract rates are charged against an allocated picture budget out of which picture rental and copyright fees must also be paid or on an hourly rate of $35–$40 per hour for searcher's time plus expenses.

Programs for libraries. Budget-conscious libraries cannot normally afford to spend money on programs. However, a few fee-based information services have successfully presented programs to library and education groups for a fee.

Adaya Henis of New Jersey charges $100 for her folk music and puppet-making programs presented to libraries.

Public relations. Libraries without a full-time public relations department occasionally hire fee-based information services at $5–$35 per hour to write press releases, feature articles for local newspapers, and patron handouts.

Alice Norton provides freelance public relations services to libraries, library systems, and library associations in Connecticut, which include mounting publicity campaigns, planning and evaluating ongoing public relations programs, writing annual reports and guides, and training staff in the fields of communication and public relations.

Publishing. "If you ask me I could write a book" go the words of an old song. Why wait until they ask you? Why not publish your own book—index, bibliography, handbook, newsletter, or directory?

I did. My firm publishes an annual directory and a bimonthly periodical. We hire writers, edit copy, market, and distribute our products ourselves. What started out a few years ago as a term paper for a library school course became for us a viable business.

Sherry Powell and Marilyn Stern did not wait for an invitation from a publisher either. They compile and distribute, through their fee-based information service, Marsh InfoServices, Inc., a directory of hot lines called *Help in a Hurry!* Because it is the only comprehensive listing of hot-line numbers in the New York metropolitan area, it fills a need unmet by commercial publishing houses.

There are numerous other examples of fee-based information services that write and successfully market their own publications.

Washington Researchers' "The Information Report," a newsletter published six times a year, gives tips to businesses on fact-finding and research techniques. FIND/SVP sells a directory of market research reports, studies, and surveys called *Findex*.

Besides providing profits from their sales, publications draw clients who make use of other services. But it is not all roses. When you make the decision to publish, you have to guarantee that your work will be profitable. You provide front money and take the risk of losing it if the project is not successful.

Purchasing service. Umbrella Associates, a fee-based information service specializing in art, offers a purchasing service. But before you conjure up romantic images of its employees rummaging through stacks of art books in search of out-of-print books, you would best be advised that in this multimedia world purchasing can mean the purchase of anything. Umbrella Associates can purchase for you a computer, library equipment, supplies, a data base, or locate a dealer or distributor and, yes, even books.

Purchasing services are offered in connection with larger jobs or as a separate service.

Quick reference service. Many fee-based information services refer a caller to the local library or provide a quick answer gratis if the question can be answered readily. Freely filling ordinary requests for correct spellings, library hours of operation (keep the local library's brochure handy), and names of sports record holders keeps everyone happy.

Often, quick reference questions put to a fee-based information service require a short but intense period of searching to provide an answer and in these cases a preestablished minimum rate of one-quarter to one-half hour of search time is charged.

Andrew Garvin of FIND/SVP says: "A quick information question for us might be how many calculators were sold in the U.S. in 1978."[4]

Facts for a Fee, a fee-based information service of the Cleveland Public Library, provides approximately 15 minutes of free time and offers the patron a fee-based information service when questions require searches beyond that limit.

Records management. Throw this out. Save that. Get rid of this. Hang on to that for at least three years. And so it goes with records management, the service of advising businesses on what to keep and why, and what to throw away and why. Similar in scope and price to consulting work.

Research. The term "research" appears on sales literature of fee-based information services. Clients understand this generic term used to describe information-gathering techniques such as on-line searching, use of information collections to gather information to answer a question, and so on.

Résumés. Who better than an ex-librarian could organize a person's life onto a single sheet of paper? Librarians trained in reference methodology are successful at résumé writing because they have the skills to draw information from a client and phrase questions so the client's responses fill information needs.

Writing the résumé is secondary to gathering the right information from an interview. In recent years many new books reflecting changes in résumé styles have been published, and fitting facts into these prescribed formats is easily learned from example.

Preparing a résumé should take about two hours, one hour spent interviewing the client and one hour writing the résumé.

Current rates for résumé preparation are $25–$50 per résumé.

Repackaging information. In theoretical discussions about fee-based information services, the question of reselling information surfaces from time to time. "What would you do," a panelist at a library conference is asked, "if you receive two identical requests for the same information? Would you resell the information to the second client at the same price you charged the first client?"

In actual practice, the situation rarely occurs, but it brings up the question of who owns the information a fee-based information service provides a client: (1) the client, (2) the fee-based information service, or (3) none of the above. The answer is (3), none of the above. Neither the client nor the fee-based information service owns the information. Information belongs to the public and is not "sold" by the fee-based information service to the client. What is sold is the expertise to gather information for a client. In the case of identical requests, the expertise required to gather information for one client is the same as for a second client and should be compensated equally in both cases.

Repackaging information occurs when a fee-based information service sees a wider market for information gathered in the course of another project. Andrew Garvin in FIND/SVP says:

> We do not do that [resell information] as a matter of course. . . . Those publications of our own that we have marketed, developed separately from any contract project that we have done. For example, we did a study on the bottled water industry which we have available as a publication but we did not actually do a full-fledged market study for an individual client. We did a lot of bottled water work.[5]

Creating a new product with additional research is a perfectly legitimate practice—it is also a smart marketing technique.

Reviews. Informally, reviews are given each time a fee-based information service provides recommendations for purchase of an item. A few fee-based information services provide formal reviews through their own information products.

Prior to the release of Library Management and Services' *Practical Law Books Review,* lawyers had to physically examine law books to make an informed decision on purchase. Now they can subscribe to the review published by this Texas (Austin) fee-based information broker.

In England, corporate librarians subscribe to *Next Month's Directories and New Business Books* and *Library and Information News,* which review books and services of interest to librarians. Both periodicals are available from London Researchers.

Selective dissemination of information. This awesome phrase, abbreviated SDI, means scanning journals, government documents, data bases, and other sources for articles on a topic preselected by a client. Furnishing the client with copies of articles of interest enables him or her to keep abreast of developments in any field without a substantial personal investment of time and money. It is, therefore, a popular service and easy to sell, especially to individuals and companies in highly technical areas.

Rates vary with the type of source used and the difficulty in obtaining copies.

Seminars and workshops. Short courses come in two varieties —those that are part of a larger project and those you market as a separate entity.

Sometimes setting aside an afternoon and declaring it a seminar is the only way to get a group of people together in the same room at the same time to discuss a common issue. For example, if you wanted to make certain that all staff members understood the operations of the information center you were hired to organize, you could: (1) send each a memo explaining its purpose and function, (2) speak to each person individually, or (3) give a short workshop.

In the case of a memo, it would probably go unread due to its nature and length. Speaking to each person individually is better, but that would take up so much of your time that your client would be faced with a large bill for your time or you would have to go uncompensated for your time and absorb the cost yourself.

A less expensive and more effective way of reaching everyone would be through a presentation and question-and-answer period. Organizing and marketing a seminar for the general public requires a substantial investment in advertising and space rental, but a few fee-based information services have been successful at selling seminars and workshops to the public as well as to other information professionals. The most notable example is Washington Researchers, which currently offers one- and two-day seminars on researching businesses, information sources in government, and finding experts. Although these topics are Washington Researchers' areas of special expertise, cofounder Matt Lesko does not feel that he is training future competitors who will also specialize in these areas. "We encourage people to do research themselves whether they are seminar participants or potential clients. . . . We haven't lost any business as a result of our policy."[6]

Speakers service. Fee-based information services function as speakers' bureaus by providing experts in various fields to conferences, panels, and conventions. Many fee-based information service owners are themselves speakers at library and information science conventions. The names Matthew Lesko, Andrew Garvin, and Susan Klement are familiar to many librarians and information professionals who have heard them address problems and issues facing the fee-based information industry.

Unfortunately, in the library/information world, speakers are often not remunerated for their services or they receive an honorarium as small as $50–$100 plus travel expenses, but speakers do accept engagements at these low rates if they feel sufficient publicity will be gained from an appearance.

Storytelling. Don't you envy Nancy Schimmel and Carol Leita? Who are these women? They are two California freelancers who travel around the country in a van, stopping to tell stories to groups of children, senior citizens, and campers. Similarly, Connie Regan and Barbara Freeman of The Folktellers not only give storytelling concerts, but also teach the art of storytelling to others.

Ah, the open road, the freedom, the sheer delight of storytelling. Of course, it is not quite that simple. Creating a storytelling hour is perhaps easier than marketing the service. Building a storytelling route takes time and much work without pay, but it can be done.

Children's and school librarians have used the direct approach of contacting festivals, universities, libraries, and radio stations to sell storytelling hours at $10–$200 per concert.

Systems design. Designing an information retrieval system is similar to organizing an information collection because it requires the analysis of information needs and provides solutions to information problems through organization, but it differs in that it involves integrating into a single system all information resources of a company—files, reports, media, library collection, and so on.

SIS of Canada cites an oil company as a typical client in need of an information system. By designing a single system, SIS could provide "easy access to files, reports, records, library materials, maps, and other materials."[7]

Rates for systems design range between $25 and $75 per hour plus expenses.

Thesaurus construction. Thesaurus construction is normally not sold as a separate service, but as a part of a larger project such as systems design or development of a computerized index.

Training. Share your wealth of knowlege with others by marketing your training products. Dale Shaffer, a library consultant from Ohio, reaches a wide audience with his own catalog of publications on various aspects of librarianship from management to improving the status of librarians.

Susan Klement of Information Resources trains potential owners/operators of fee-based information services through short courses at graduate schools of library science in the United States and Canada. Golden Adams teaches genealogy to students in Utah. Jodi Simpson tutors potential indexers.

What is your expertise? Share it through training others.

Translating. Not normally sold as a separate service, but offered by many fee-based information services. If you feel you will be called on to translate technical materials, get the names of foreign-language experts from the local university and keep them handy for future jobs.

Verifying facts. Writers and publishers hire fee-based information services to check manuscripts for accuracy. This service is sold on an hourly or contract basis.

Writing. What do fee-based information service owners/operators write? Training manuals, technical reports, articles for library and information journals, newspaper articles, guidelines, handbooks—in short, just about anything.

NOTES

1. Washington Researchers promotional materials.
2. Author's conversations with Matthew Lesko, Washington Researchers.
3. Author's conversations with Rosemary Eakins, Research Reports.
4. "Profile," *Journal of Fee-Based Information Services* 1, no. 6 (November/December 1979): 10.
5. Ibid., pp. 11-12.
6. Ibid. 2, no. 1 (January/February 1980): 7.
7. Ibid. 2, no. 2 (March/April 1980): 8.

THE BUSINESS OF RUNNING A BUSINESS

Unlike working in a library or most other places of employment, where you receive a regular paycheck for the hours you are at work—including times when there is little to do, staff meetings or conferences away from the job, lunch hours, and coffee breaks, plus extra pay for overtime—there is no guarantee with a fee-based information service that you will be financially rewarded for the time you spend working in your company.

Running a fee-based information service is like running any other business—you are paid according to the money you earn, in this case, the money you collect from your clients. It is possible to work at a fee-based information service fewer than 35 or 40 hours a week and earn a lot of money, possibly much more than you now earn. It is also possible to offer excellent service to clients large and small, work hard from 9 to 5 or later in the evening Monday through Friday and a few Saturdays every month, and not earn any money at all and perhaps lose money—if you do not manage your business well.

MANAGEMENT—THE KEY

Poor management or lack of awareness about how to manage a business leads to erosion of profits and ineffective use of employees' time. Managing a business well means, in essence, being aware of the rules of business: realizing that you must make a profit to stay in business, that you must use your time well, and that you must plan for the future.

77

As an example of a poorly managed although potentially successful business, let us look at a fee-based information service now six months old. The owner, the company's only full-time employee, puts in between 40 and 50 hours a week running the business and serving the needs of her clients. Although she works full time, she is not earning enough money to support herself, and she has had to dip into her savings account more than she would like just to pay her bills. Although she loves her work, she is now beginning to wonder how she will be able to stay in business in the future.

How does this owner manage her service? Let us look at a day-by-day account of the company's operation during a typical week.

Monday. The owner spent all day at a university library doing a manual search for a small engineering firm. She had been employed by the library for five years before starting her own service and still has many friends there. One of them, a reference librarian, asked her to lunch, and their conversation about the past and about their current lives ran past the lunch hour and into the early afternoon, which is a slow period in the reference department.

Tuesday. The owner returned to the library to finish the search; she left by noon, but not before she ran into her old boss, who asked her to return the following week to replace a librarian on vacation. As a favor to the director, she agreed to work at a rate equivalent to her old salary. After lunch she made cold calls on two potential clients.

Wednesday. In the morning the owner advised a small professional firm on designing an information collection. Then she had lunch and spent the afternoon hunting down a journal article for a document delivery job.

Thursday. The owner spent the morning on a current awareness job for a new client. The project took longer than she expected because the field was larger than she had anticipated. That evening she prepared a report on the consulting job.

Friday. The owner had planned to start work organizing an information collection for a new client, but earlier in the week the company called to cancel the project. This left her with a little unplanned time, so she decided to save the money she would ordinarily pay a typist to type the short report on the consulting job and do it herself. Because she is a slow typist, it took her the better part of the day to complete a clean final copy for delivery to the client. She spent the balance of the day on bookkeeping chores, billing clients and posting expenses to her ledgers.

The owner's total earnings for the week amounted to $260, which is less than she had earned at her old job, but still a livable wage and a respectable sum for a business in existence only six months. At that rate she should earn more than $1,000 per month (see Gross Earnings table).

So, why does this owner have to dip into her savings account to make ends meet?

Gross Earnings
$150   (consulting 3 hours @ $50)
10   (document delivery)
25   (current awareness)
75   (manual search)
$260 per week × 4 weeks per month = $1,040 per month

Part of the answer lies in the cost of operating her business. She cannot accurately claim an income of $1,040 because she has not deducted monthly operating expenses (rent, utility bills, telephone, answering service) plus one-twelfth of her yearly cost of supplies, postage, clerical assistance, and other overhead. Her total operating expenses average $495, which means she has earned $505, not $1,040.

At that rate her projected income for the year will be only $6,060 (see Operating Costs table). No wonder she has had to supplement her earnings with money from her savings account!

What can the owner do to earn more money? First, she must estimate the amount of money she needs to earn so that she can establish a fee structure that will allow her to reach her financial goal. She will add to her annual operating expenses her desired personal income plus fringe benefits. (When you are on your own, you have to provide for your own medical and dental insurance, pension plan, sick days, vacation, and other benefits.)

Let us say she comes up with a total financial need of $30,000 per year. That may sound high for a beginner, but remember that this is not her actual salary because she must allow for operating expenses and fringe benefits.

Operating Costs

Monthly Cost	Expense
$200	rent (she has allocated 1 room in her 2-room apartment for her business; her rent is $400 per month)
80	phone (average monthly bill for business phone)
60	utilities (heating, electricity, etc., again ½ of her bill)
30	answering service
25	postage (1/12 of the estimated $300 spent annually)
50	supplies (1/12 of the estimated $600 spent annually)
50	clerical assistance (1/12 of the estimated $600 spent annually)

$495 total monthly operating expenses × 12 months = $6,060 per year

To determine an average hourly rate, she must divide the $30,000 figure by the number of hours she intends to work for clients during the year. Based on a 40-hour work week with two weeks annual vacation, it would appear that her average hourly fee should be $15 (see Assumed Billable Hours table).

She cannot, however, depend on 40 billable hours (hours she charges clients) a week because she must take into consideration that she will spend 20 to 50 percent or 8 to 20 hours a week seeking clients and generally promoting her business, hours for which she will not be paid.

She must also plan on spending another 20 percent or eight hours a week managing her business, supervising her part-time help, ironing out problems, and planning, hours for which she will not be paid.

In addition, she will not be paid for the time she spends writing proposals and figuring estimates for jobs she may or may not take on. Nor will she be paid for lunch hours and rest breaks or for the time she loses commuting to jobs or information sources.

The amount of time she bills to clients varies from week to week. Next week when she fills in at the university library she will bill her client for 40 hours. Some weeks, when she gathers background materials and prepares detailed proposals for potential jobs, she will not bill any time at all.

Assumed Billable Hours (per week)

$$40 \text{ hours per week}$$
$$\underline{\times\ 50 \text{ weeks per year}}$$
$$2,000 \text{ hours per year}$$

$$\$30,000 \text{ income package}$$
$$\underline{\div\quad 2,000 \text{ hours per year}}$$

$$\$15 \text{ per hour}$$

Figuring an average throughout the year of 45 percent of her time spent as billable time, or 18 hours per week, her average fee to clients must be $33 per hour, or $600 per week (see Actual Billable Hours table).

Can a fee-based information service charge $33 per hour or more plus expenses? Yes, most definitely, yes. Fee-based information services charge $35, $50, or more per hour.

You, too, can charge these amounts because the services you will offer are worth it. Women more than men sometimes tend to feel guilty about charging high hourly rates when they begin a business, and they may underprice their services as a result. Some women who work part-time feel that they must charge even less simply because they are not employed in the field full-time.

Do not let guilt keep you from charging what you are worth. Just look at what your competition charges to get an idea of what you should charge and raise your rates to meet theirs if necessary.

The owner in our example spent approximately 60 percent of her time working for clients during that week, but she earned less than one-half of her financial goal for that period. Why? Let us look at her week again and offer some suggestions as to how she can make a profit, use her time more effectively, and plan for the future success of her business.

In our example, the owner earned $75 for a manual search, $10 to deliver a document, $150 for consulting, and $25 for current awareness, for a total of $260. Her fees, which are a bit low compared with those of her competitors, are nonetheless respectable. What is at fault is the amount of time she took on each job.

By learning to put her time to better use, she will increase her profits and spend less time working.

Actual Billable Hours (per week)

$$18 \text{ hours per week}$$
$$\times\ 50 \text{ weeks per year}$$

$$900 \text{ hours per year}$$

$$\$30,000$$
$$\div\ 900 \text{ hours}$$

$$\$33 \text{ per hour}$$

$$18 \text{ hours per week}$$
$$\times\ \$33 \text{ per hour}$$

$$\$594 \text{ needed financial}$$
$$\text{goal per week}$$

MANUAL SEARCH

The owner of our fee-based information service certainly cannot afford to spend an entire day and half of the next, as she did on Monday and Tuesday, for a job that will pay only $75. Because she spoke with a friend for part of the day on Monday, her actual billable time was closer to 8 hours than to 12, which would make her hourly fee about $9.37 per hour, or less than the one-third of her needed hourly goal of $33 per hour.

Realistically she could not have charged her client $33 per hour, for a total of $264, for a job that was worth only $75. So, instead of spending eight hours on a manual search, she could have spent a few minutes on the phone to an on-line searching service describing the parameters of the search and tacked on a small charge to her client for her part in the project. Both she and her client would have been better off because the on-line connect time plus her fee would probably have been less than $75.

An on-line search is not always the most expedient way to search, but in some cases it is better to subcontract to another service than it is to spend hours searching manually.

While she would probably have earned less than $75 by subcontracting the job, she would have been free on Monday and Tuesday morning to accept another job.

DOCUMENT DELIVERY

She could have subcontracted the document delivery job as well and earned a few dollars, but, more important, gained three additional hours on Wednesday.

Another alternative to spending three hours and earning $10, or less than the minimum wage, would be to reconsider accepting small jobs such as this one in the first place. Some fee-based information services set a minimum charge of $25 or $50 and will not perform a small document delivery job for less than the minimum.

Others offer retainers to encourage clients to use their services more frequently and give discounts on document delivery jobs to clients who pay the monthly fee and call in on an as-needed basis. Although this does not reduce the search time to locate a document, it does encourage a client to use your service more frequently since it has already paid for service.

CONSULTING

Earning $150 for three hours' consulting is not bad. But did the owner really spend only three hours on the job?

Let us not talk about the time she spent seeking the job, or the amount of time she spent gathering background information in preparation for the job. Let us just talk about actual time on the job. She was in the client's office for three hours, spent two hours at home writing a report, and three hours typing it. Total number of hours spent on the job—eight. Average hourly fee—$18.75.

She should have considered the time she spent writing the report as part of her services and charged the client for five hours instead of two and added the cost of a typist's fee to the bill.

Her theory in typing the report herself was that it would save her money, while, in effect, she lost $33 for each hour she spent typing the report instead of working for a client.

CURRENT AWARENESS

Before committing herself to providing current awareness to her new client, the owner estimated a monthly charge of $25 based on 45 minutes of work a month. After she began the project, she realized she had underestimated the size of the field covered in the request and would have to spend three hours each month on the job rather than the three-quarters of an hour she had allocated originally. Still, she charged only $25.

On the one hand, she felt angry with herself at having misjudged the amount of time, but on the other hand she felt guilty about asking the client for more money after she quoted the $25 figure, even though she realized that the amount of time she must spend on the job had tripled.

What the owner fails to realize is that an estimate is only an approximation of costs, not a final figure. Although she cannot go ahead with the project and exceed the estimate without her client's approval, she should go back to the client and explain the situation as soon as possible.

The client can then authorize her to go ahead with the full project at a higher rate or ask her to perform a limited service within the framework of the original estimate. Or the client can reject the project entirely.

The owner has not made a mistake so she should not be afraid to ask for more money, nor should she assume the client will say no. Accurately estimating jobs is very difficult, even for people who have been doing it for a while. Just think about the last time you took your car in for repairs. Unless it was in writing, was your mechanic's estimate on the nose?

Not asking for an equitable sum and going ahead with a full project for a low rate will only jeopardize the client relationship in the future because the client will assume that the owner will perform services at low, low rates and be surprised if she charges her normal rate.

TEMPORARY REPLACEMENT

Next week the owner will work as a temporary replacement librarian at the university library where she used to work. Her weekly earnings will amount to $300, which is the same wage she earned as a permanent librarian and more than is earned by the librarian she is replacing. Both she and the director feel it is a fair agreement.

Although she can use the ready money and welcomes the brief return to the regular world of nine to five as a change of routine, perhaps she should think twice about accepting the job. Besides spending 100 percent of her time working for a client and earning only half her weekly financial goal of $600, she will be tied up all week at the university library and unable to promote her business or take care of her duties as a manager. The job will do little to enhance her reputation, and perhaps she will even desire to return to the library after spending a week in familiar surroundings.

On the other hand, she may be reminded of the reasons she left to start her own business and be anxious to get back to running it.

NONBILLABLE HOURS

Equally important as the way the owner spends her time working for clients is how she spends her time working for herself.

Friday afternoon usually finds her bent over a set of financial books, fingers working the keys of a calculator. Because of a cash-flow problem, she feels she cannot wait until the end of the month to bill her clients and prefers instead to do her bookkeeping once a week.

At the same time she prepares invoices, she posts her expenses and receipts to her ledgers. Instead of lumping together the separate tasks of billing and posting, she should post daily and bill once a month. By doing her bookkeeping four times a month as she does now, she wastes time that is better spent promoting business or working for clients.

Posting daily saves time spent trying to remember how many miles she drove in connection with jobs and what that little scrap of paper with "$5.95 paid in full" refers to. Until now she has been lax about posting expenses because she has not wanted to trouble her clients with small amounts. But if she does not start charging for photocopies, mileage, and the like, she will find these little amounts taking a large chunk out of her annual earnings.

Billing once a month will cut down on her invoicing time because she will write only one bill per client per month instead of one bill per job as she does now. She can further reduce her time by setting a minimum billing amount of $50 and asking for all amounts under $50 to be paid in advance.

Her reason for billing each week, to collect money quickly, has failed to produce any results because her clients seldom pay immediately after receiving a bill, and she is reluctant to jeopardize a relationship by dunning a client.

If she does not want to act the part of a bill collector, she can still get her clients to pay on time each month by adding the phrase "payable within 10 days" and imposing a late fee of a few dollars for each ten days the bill remains unpaid. While the fee will be small, psychologically a late fee shows her clients that she is serious about getting paid.

Another tactic that will help her cash-flow problem is to ask for a nonrefundable deposit of one-third to one-half her estimated fee, thereby giving her money to work with while performing a job.

Had she done this on the collection organizing project that was called off by the client, perhaps the client would have thought twice about calling off a job that was almost paid for. Had the client still canceled the project, she should have no qualms about keeping the deposit since she had already put work into preparation for the job.

PROMOTION

Although the owner is headed in the right direction as far as promotion is concerned by using a variety of techniques to seek new clients—in the typical week we saw her make cold calls, use word of mouth—she must free herself to spend more time promoting her business to reach enough potential clients to stay in business.

By using her billable hours more effectively, she will create more time to promote her business.

TIME WASTERS

The most obvious example of time wasted by our sample owner is the time spent talking to a friend at the library. Rather than taking time away from her work day, she could have invited her friend to dinner or visited her at the library on a Saturday. Were she in the habit of keeping a time log, she would have seen how much time she lost talking with her friend and had an accurate record of time spent on the project.

There are less obvious examples. Since she must have lunch out often during the week, instead of dining alone or with a friend she can turn the lunch hour into an informal sales meeting with a prospective client. Meeting for lunch creates an informal atmosphere conducive to selling.

Perhaps this conjures up in your mind images of a fancy restaurant and a client being plied with wine. In reality, sales luncheons are generally far away from this image. Not all people drink at lunch and most do not expect to be taken to the Ritz. Any respectable restaurant within a short drive or walk from the client's office will do.

Besides taking potential clients to lunch, she can use her lunch hour to interview experts in connection with research or meet other information professionals with whom she plans informal working arrangements.

In addition to creating more time for herself, she will also create a tax deduction since business entertaining is a legitimate expense. Of course, inviting another person to lunch doubles the bill, but without the second lunch her meal is not deductible.

LOOKING TO THE FUTURE

Our owner is so consumed by day-to-day activities that she has not had time to think about where she is going and what she will do once she gets there. Although she drew up a sound business plan before she started her business, having reached a six-month milestone it is now time for plan B.

Now is the time to think about the future. Her business plan need not be as detailed as the plan she drew up when she designed her business, but she should have at least a mental plan or a short plan on paper to take out and look at from time to time. She needs to sit down for a while and brainstorm about where she would like to be next year, five years from now, ten years from now.

Does she want to stay self-employed? Or hire employees? Is her goal to earn a lot of money so she can afford some of the better things life has to offer? Or would she rather position herself to earn a livable wage through part-time work so she can pursue her avocation of travel? Should she develop a specialty?

Her plan will also help her determine whether she will have to return to school to learn new skills, decide whether she really wants to be her own boss or return to working for someone else.

BASIC QUESTIONS AND ANSWERS

Q. What is the key to success in the fee-based information service?

A. Good management.

Q. How can you improve your business management?

A. By learning to put your business time to better use, such as figuring out how much of your work week is spent as billable time.

Q. What should you do if you discover that the actual time you must spend on a project far exceeds your original estimate?

A. Explain the situation to the client immediately, who can then approve the project at a higher rate, ask you to perform limited service within the original estimate, or reject the project.

GETTING SMART

Training for a career in a fee-based information service does not end with a master's degree in library science or some other related area. As your business grows and changes, you will want—and need—to pick up new skills and brush up old ones.

Where to turn? Graduate schools of library science, library associations, business schools, community colleges, business associations, and periodicals offer continuing education of value to the owner/operator of a fee-based information service.

GRADUATE SCHOOLS OF LIBRARY SCIENCE

Although few graduate schools of library science identify a core concentration for potential owners and operators of fee-based information services, many allow students to create their own concentration from individual courses.

Among the courses of special value are those in computer science and data bases. Dalhousie University School of Library Service (Halifax, Nova Scotia), for example, offers as noncredit courses COBOL programming and FORTRAN programming in preparation for a three-hour seminar, "Computers and Information Systems," in which students design an information system. At Simmons College Graduate School of Library and Information Science (Boston, Massachusetts), "On-line Data Bases" covers the basics of bibliographic data bases. The school describes the course thus:

Examines computerized information retrieval, focusing on bibliographic data bases. Emphasizes developing the student's competency in translating the patron's information need into an effective strategy, and then using that strategy to search on-line data bases. . . . A data base and computer search program will be developed in class.[1]

Courses in indexing and abstracting, whether or not they explore computerized methods, provide practical skills with a variety of applications to fee-based information services. Florida State University School of Library Science (Tallahassee) offers "Abstracting and Indexing," a five-credit course in which students study "design, operation, and evaluation of abstracting and indexing systems" and receive "practice in abstracting and indexing techniques."[2]

Basic to fee-based information services is a course in records management. At McGill University Graduate School of Library Science (Montreal) records management is taught through lectures, presentations, and projects that explore the management, storage, and protection of information within organizations. The course includes an examination of word processing, micrographics, and the impact of technology on records management.

Special courses organize into a neat package the literature of a single subject or the management of an information collection in a single subject. Special literature and special library courses taught by U.S. and Canadian library schools are available with few exceptions to all students. In the areas of medical or legal librarianship, courses are sometimes restricted to students formally enrolled in a program leading to certification or licensing by a professional organization.

A special bibliography course given at the University of Wisconsin–Milwaukee School of Library Science rotates each semester among topics including film, criminal justice, ethnic literature, and others. Students can accumulate up to nine credits in special bibliography.

At the University of Toronto Faculty of Library Science, a student can choose from among several "special materials" courses including map librarianship, music librarianship, and research collections in Canadiana.

Queens College of the City University of New York Department of Library Science combines special librarianship with special bibliography in its series "Information Sources and Services." After completing "Information Sources and Services: General," a study of general information sources, students are eligible for "Science and Technology," "Social Science," "Humanities or Information Sources," and "Visual Arts."

At the University of California, Berkeley, "Law Librarianship: Legal Research, Reference and Bibliography" is a three-credit course available to third-year law students and all students enrolled in the School of Library and Information Studies. It includes:

> [An] Introduction to legal bibliography; cases and reports, statutes, administrative regulations and decisions, legislative history, legal citators and digests, legal periodicals and indexes, secondary materials, legal bibliography tools.[3]

Related to law librarianship are government documents courses. At Emory University Division of Librarianship (Atlanta), government documents are covered by "Governmental Information Systems," which studies "information production by governments and strategies for access to this information. Emphasis on the federal government with some attention to state and local."[4] At Kent State University School of Library Science (Kent, Ohio), the emphasis in its "Government Documents" course is on "U.S. publications, municipal and state publications, and major documents of Great Britain, Canada, and United Nations."[5]

Of obvious value are courses in business librarianship. "Management of Business Information" at Rosary College Graduate School of Library Science (River Forest, Illinois) provides "an introduction to the concept, organization, and management of business libraries and to the use of basic information sources and data bases in business."[6] At Simmons College Graduate School of Library and Information Science, "Introduction to Business Literature" discusses "marketing, finance, banking, accounting and control, production and operation management, industrial relations, transportation, and logistics."[7] Professor Robert Burgess includes a unit on freelance librarianship in his course "Library

Service to the Business Community" at the State University of New York School of Library and Information Science (Albany).

At the University of Iowa School of Library Science (Iowa City), information brokering is taught as a unit in a course on special libraries.

Independent study courses offer a student a chance to conduct a market study of a community in terms of starting a fee-based information service. The assistant dean of the University of Kentucky College of Library Science (Lexington), James Sodt, reported to Information Alternative that he supervised an independent study marketing analysis of the Northern Greater Cincinnati area. While a student at the State University of New York School of Library and Information Science, Susan R. LaForte of the Springfield (Massachusetts) City Library completed a paper on information brokers entitled "Information Brokering: A New Direction for Librarians?"

Some library schools encourage students formally enrolled in master of library science (MLS) programs to take elective courses in other departments, especially computer and business departments, if they intend to open fee-based information services.

At the University of California–Los Angeles Graduate School of Library and Information Science, it is possible to earn an MLS and a master of business administration (MBA) in three years by enrolling in a joint degree program sponsored by the Graduate School of Library and Information Science and the Graduate School of Management.

> Normally, this involves a year of course work in each of the two schools, in which the basic professional competencies in management and in library and information science are successively obtained. The program then is completed by a third year of course work, internship and field-work study, and a specialization paper that satisfies the requirements of both programs.[8]

Rosary College's joint MBA/MALS program requires a total of 54 semester hours, with a minimum of 30 semester hours taken in the Graduate School of Library Science and a minimum of 24 semester hours taken in the Master of Business Administration program.

Syracuse University School of Information Studies (New York) developed a new degree, Master of Science in Information Resources Management (MS/IRM), recommended for, among others, information counselors. It requires 54 credit hours, including a core of 27 credits in the area of information management and systems, 21 credit electives, and a seminar in which students produce a lengthy research paper. Included among possible electives are such business courses as "Managerial Behavior," "The Management Process," and "Organization Theory," and public administration courses such as "Quantitative Aids to Policy Analysis," "Public Budgeting," and "Intergovernmental Relations."

Syracuse University School of Information Studies is one school that pays more than lip service to the idea of information brokering. In the 1979–1980 *Bulletin*, it devoted space to describing what an information broker does and ended the description with:

> A decision to work as an independent information broker requires some capital for support in the beginning, an ability to take risks, a certain amount of chutzpah, and a belief in one's capabilities.[9]

The University of Pittsburgh Graduate School of Library and Information Sciences also mentions information brokers in its publications and offers students a variety of up-to-date courses in information studies, although none tailored to information brokers.

One of the few schools of library science that identifies a track of studies for the potential owner/operator of a fee-based information service is McGill University Graduate School of Library Science. In its unpublished "Courses for Careers: Guidelines," a core of courses plus suggested electives are mentioned for various concentrations. The core consists of "Selection and Use of Books and Related Materials," "Reference Materials and Methods I and II," "Introduction to Organization of Materials," "Technical Services," "Introduction to Data Processing," "Research Methods," "Information Facility Management," and "Introduction to the Information Environment."

Suggested electives for information consultants/brokers are "Advanced Organization of Materials," "Systems Analysis," "Library Automation and Networks," "Information Retrieval," "Indexing," and "Issues in Information."

Suggested electives for researchers/information workers are "Information Retrieval," "Indexing," "Scientific and Technical

Literature," "Business Literature," "Reference Services in the Humanities and Social Sciences," "Government Publications," "Biomedical Librarianship," and "Law Librarianship."

Why do so few library schools identify a track of studies for the potential owner/operator of a fee-based information service? In a survey conducted by Information Alternative of library schools in the United States and Canada, two library school deans provided an answer.

In reply to the survey's question, "What courses do you offer potential information brokers?" one dean responded:

> This specialization corresponds to what we call a "type of library" orientation, and our curriculum is not set up along these lines. Many of our courses contain materials, skills, and concepts that are appropriate for students considering careers in information brokerage and other nonlibrary markets for information professionals. Students with a definite interest in information brokerage are encouraged to pursue this orientation in their term papers and other elective assignments. We have also made a practice of inviting information brokers to come to talk to our classes.[10]

In answer to the survey question, "Do you offer a concentration to potential brokers similar to those offered to potential school librarians, public librarians, special librarians, etc.?" the reply from another dean was:

> No, but I am not in favor of type of library concentration. That ` implies that information is institution bound, which it is not.[11]

In responding to the Information Alternative survey, a third dean shed a slightly different light on the matter of training potential owners/operators of fee-based information services. His comments were:

> If a student completes the courses in information science and related library science courses and if that student can take some independent study and research courses on information brokerage, and if he or she can take courses in the School of Business Administration especially those in accounting, marketing, small business management, etc., and if he/she is ambitious, aggressive (in the good sense) and wants to make money,

willing to take risks, energetic, outgoing and articulate, chances are that he/she will enter the field of information brokerage. Whether or not he/she will succeed depends on other external factors such as "good luck" or being at the right place at the right time or having the proper contacts. The previous "if's" show that to a large extent the courses are there, but we need a new breed of students who are willing to enter the new field of information brokerage. We also need to strengthen contacts between library schools and the information brokers who have been successful in their endeavors.[12]

SHORT COURSES AND WORKSHOPS

Short courses and workshops sponsored by graduate schools of library science provide training for potential owners/operators of fee-based information services.

Susan Klement, owner of Information Resources in Toronto, Canada, gave a workshop on career alternatives to summer students enrolled at Kent State University School of Library Science. Topics included "range of nontraditional jobs; the floating librarian; special libraries versus librarians without libraries; records management; information as a commodity; freelance librarianship and information brokerage; fees for service; running a business; obtaining money; presenting oneself."[13] The week-long course entitled "Workshop: Career Alternatives in Librarianship" was offered on a credit/noncredit basis.

Syracuse University School of Information Studies has conducted two workshops for information brokers and freelance librarians.

In 1976, Maxine Davis of the now defunct Information Access (Syracuse) moderated a one-day workshop called "Information Broker/Freelance Librarian—New Careers—New Library Services" held at a hall off campus from Syracuse University.

Representing the small fee-based information services sector, Susan Klement fielded questions from the audience—"How did you get started?" "What is your income" "What do you charge?" and so on.

Christopher Samuels, whose Information for Business was started with a capital investment of several hundred thousand dollars, described his early days in a corporate library where he was reprimanded for wearing a blue shirt instead of the required white, and went on to talk about the workings of a large fee-based information service.

The establishment of a fee-based information service at the Minneapolis Public Library was described in depth by Carol Vantine, who at the time of the workshop was employed by INFORM, Minneapolis Public Library's fee-based information service. Although some of the information is now outdated and there have been personnel changes (Carol Vantine is no longer at INFORM; Information for Business has undergone changes), the proceedings of the workshop, available through the university's publications office, are still of value to anyone thinking of starting a fee-based information service.

"Alternative Careers in Information Library Services" was the title of Syracuse's 1977 workshop, also coordinated by Maxine Davis. The two-day workshop addressed such issues as how to start a fee-based information service and careers for librarians in nonlibrary settings. A summary of the proceedings of this workshop is also available through the publications office.

In a similar vein, the University of Maryland College of Library and Information Services conducted a workshop in 1980 entitled "Workshop on Lucrative Librarianship." Topics discussed included basic tax information, marketing, planning, client relationships, and other areas of concern to the information entrepreneur.

In the spring of 1981, the State University of New York at Albany School of Library and Information Science sponsored, in connection with Information Alternative and Info/motion, a two-day workshop on information brokering. Alice Sizer Warner, consultant, owner of The Information Guild and cofounder of Warner-Eddison Associates, Inc., spoke on identifying a market and keeping clients. Matthew Lesko of Washington Researchers discussed the use of experts as a means of gathering information. The "who, what, why, and how" of information brokering was given by Barbara Felicetti of Info/motion. Information brokering within the corporation was the topic discussed by Gerry Radway of General Electric. Kelly Warnken of Information Alternative identified sources of assistance for information brokers. Also discussed were the financial and legal basics of setting up a small business and developing a graphic identity.

Although not directed at fee-based information service owners/ operators, Pratt Institute's (Brooklyn, N.Y.) seminar "Designing and Marketing Information Products and Services," in fall 1980, was valuable to anyone involved in information packaging, including, of course, fee-based information services.

LIBRARY AND INFORMATION ASSOCIATION CONFERENCES

Library and information associations seem to have finished their debate on fee vs. free and either laid the subject to rest or begun to offer workshops at conventions supporting the operation of fee-based information services. At the New York Library Association annual convention in 1980, Patricia Glass Schuman was invited to speak on the subject of alternative careers, the same subject as that of a book published by her firm, Neal-Schuman Publisher, Inc., entitled *What Else You Can Do with a Library Degree*.

During the National Information Conference and Exposition IV, sponsored by the Information Industry Association and Associated Information Managers, Barbara Whyte Felicetti presented a workshop, "Do It Yourself Business Kit: Getting Started in Small Business." A panel of three experts offered advice for small business managers and potential information brokers regarding financial, marketing, and public relations strategies. Martin White, director of Creative Strategies, Inc., London, served on a panel addressing "Marketing Information Management" in which several strategies were discussed.

It is often not necessary to belong to an association to attend a conference, and although fees are higher for nonmembers, it is often worth the extra money to receive this type of continuing education.

INFORMATION COURSES

Short courses in information-gathering techniques are beginning to pop up in continuing education divisions of universities and colleges, private schools, business schools, and private companies. These short courses provide a low-cost option and require a minimum investment of time.

Allen Todd, author of *Finding Facts Fast* (Morrow, 1972), currently teaches a short course in information-gathering techniques at New York University's Continuing Education Department. In a similar vein, Barbara Charton, research librarian for the Reader's Digest Editorial Research Department, conducts a course entitled "How to Get Information: Research Skills" at Womanschool, a private institution in Manhattan. The eight-week course is designed to cover:

[a] wide range of information needs, from the job of the administrative assistant who must find quick, factual "answers," to the longer, extensive research demands of the writer, professional researcher, or report-writing businessperson. . . . A working knowledge of various research resources (libraries, reference works, professional research services, databanks, etc.) will be acquired by students willing actively to participate in the game of getting information.[14]

Ann Novotny and Rosemary Eakins of Research Reports teach the craft of picture research at various schools in the Northeast, including Radcliffe College (Cambridge, Massachusetts). Their ten-week course "Careers: The Picture Researcher," given each fall at the International Center of Photography, is described as follows:

This course examines the specialized training and functions of professional picture researchers, who locate and edit photographs and other visual materials (engravings, woodcuts, paintings) for use in books and magazines, feature films and television, exhibitions and advertisements. Other professionals —designers, art editors, photo consultants, photographers and photo agents, legal experts, curators of archives, film producers—will discuss how their profession interrelates with the work of the picture researcher.[15]

Other owners/operators of fee-based information services also teach short courses in their areas of expertise, including Golden V. Adams, Jr., genealogy, and Jodi Simpson, indexing. Washington Researchers currently offers one- and two-day seminars on using experts, finding information on companies, and how to find information in Washington.

ON-LINE TRAINING

Familiarity with commercially produced data bases can be obtained easily through a variety of sources.

Producers such as Lockheed Information Systems' DIALOG offer frequent half-day and full-day seminars throughout the country. Currently DIALOG offers training seminars in the following areas:

System Seminar (Introductory)	1½ days
Refresher (Advanced)	½ day
Search Strategy	½ day
Humanities	½ day
Biosciences	½ day
Business	½ day
Chemistry	½ day
Chemistry (Advanced)	1 day
Excerpta Medica	½ day
Government Documents	½ day
Legal Information	½ day
Nonbibliographic Databases	½ day
Patents	½ day
Sci-Tech	½ day
Social Sciences	½ day

Fees for half-day seminars start at $25. If no seminars are scheduled in your area on the topic you wish to explore, it is possible for you to host a seminar and receive free admission for yourself and another person. The only requirements are that you provide an overhead projector, telephone lines, a terminal, and a room large enough to hold 25 people. A seminar can be cohosted by your company and a local business or university, which provides the terminal and receives in exchange free publicity and one complimentary admission.

Annual conventions such as the National Online Information Meeting, sponsored by *Online Review,* offer exhibits and lectures of interest to the potential owner/operator of a fee-based information service. The 1981 meeting held in New York City included a lecture by Alan Metter entitled "Starting an Information Retrieval Company: Some Practical Considerations," in which he described the beginnings of his company, Data-Search; a paper by Tim LaBorie of Drexel University (Philadelphia) on data bases for information professionals; and many other lectures by professionals in the data-base field.

Computer science, technology, and management colleges of universities periodically conduct short courses on data bases. For example, the American University in Washington, D.C., frequently offers a seminar on federal information sources. The spring 1981 seminar "Federal Databases: Identification, Evaluation and Access" addressed the availability and use of and access to federal data bases.

BUSINESS COURSES

To make your business venture a success, you will need to know a lot about running a small business. Much information about the world of business is available and it is not necessary to enroll in a formal business school program to become knowledgeable about the workings of a small business. Independent schools, private companies, and associations offer much in the way of quick courses for the potential small business owner.

The Womanschool (New York City) is an example of one of the many grass-roots schools organized to offer basic skills to potential business owners. Its current catalog lists many short courses of 1 to 10 sessions for less than $100, including "Effective Speaking," a 10-session course for women in business; "Math Made Manageable: The Basics," and "Applying Math Methods to Business," two math-anxiety courses; "Professional Sales Skills"; "Publicity Techniques: An Intensive Workshop"; and "Time Management." All courses are taught by professional men and women from the New York area.

In San Francisco, the New School for Democratic Management offers several 10-week courses for $90 each in the areas of "Starting a Business," "Financial Planning and Management," "Financial Development," "Democratic Management and Organizational Growth," and "Women in Business." In addition to courses offered in San Francisco, the school also has held courses in Austin, Boston, Milwaukee, and Seattle.

The most popular seminar leader in the area of consulting is Howard L. Shenson, whose short courses are conducted frequently in various cities around the country. A day-long seminar includes how to build a clientele, how to market consulting skills, how to obtain government contracts, and more. Although not specifically designed for the library/information consultant, general guidelines taught in the seminar do apply to consultants in many fields.

Women's professional business associations offer inexpensive afternoon or evening programs for the potential business owner. For example, the Los Angeles chapter of Women in Communications presented "Developing an Entrepreneurial Spirit for Your Professional Goals: How to Make Your Boss Your Client" with, as its keynote speaker, Sandra Winston, author of *The Entrepreneurial Woman* (Bantam, 1979) and founder of Women in Business, Inc., a management consulting firm.

Banks are also getting into the act of providing business training. The Chase Manhattan Bank offers its customers for $36 a membership in The Chase Exchange™, which entitles members to attendance at weekly financial seminars, personal counseling, and a newsletter, plus more information about Chase Manhattan than is desired by most people.

Although budget cuts have forced the Small Business Administration to stop its one-day workshops for women in small business, it still offers personal counseling to the potential small business owner as well as several free and low-cost publications. These tiny pamphlets, which can be read in whole on a lunch hour, provide basic information applicable to all businesses. Because the pamphlets are not normally written by government writers, they avoid jargon. For example, "Budgeting in a Small Service Firm," a Small Business Administration pamphlet by Phyllis A. Barker, associate professor of accounting at Indiana State University, starts out by explaining in plain English what a budget is and why one is necessary before setting rules for budgeting.

CURRENT AWARENESS AND SELECTIVE DISSEMINATION OF INFORMATION (SDI)

It would hardly seem necessary to have to remind potential owners/operators of fee-based information services of the importance of current awareness and SDI in the areas of information and business, but, surprisingly, this area is often neglected by information professionals who, like others, have difficulty keeping abreast of developments in their own fields.

Fortunately, you will not have to pay someone to provide you with these services (although paying another fee-based information service is certainly an option) because you have the skill and resources to organize your own current awareness program and locate copies of documents for your files.

It would also appear unnecessary to remind potential owners/ operators of fee-based information services that reading articles in library/information and business periodicals, proceedings of meetings and conferences in business and library/information, and bibliographies is one of the least expensive forms of continuing education—but it does not hurt to mention it either.

BASIC QUESTIONS AND ANSWERS

Q. Where can an information broker pick up new skills or brush up on old ones?

A. Graduate schools of library science, business schools and associations, community colleges, and periodicals.

Q. What is one course no information broker should be without?

A. Records management.

Q. How can one pick up knowledge on commercially produced data bases?

A. Such producers as Lockheed Information Systems' DIALOG offer half-day and full-day seminars throughout the country.

NOTES

1. Simmons College Graduate School of Library and Information Science, Boston, 1980/1982 *Catalog*, p. 23.
2. Florida State University, Tallahassee, School of Library Science, *Bulletin*, p. 17.
3. University of California, Berkeley, vol. 74, no. 6, June 1980 *Bulletin*, p. 12.
4. Emory University, Atlanta, Division of Librarianship, "Course Descriptions," p. 3.
5. Kent State University, Kent, Ohio, School of Library Science, "Introducing Library Science 1979–80," p. 15.
6. Rosary College, River Forest, Ill., Graduate School of Library Science, *Bulletin*, p. 21.

7. Simmons College, *Catalog*, p. 22.
8. University of California–Los Angeles, Graduate School of Library and Information Science, 1980–1981 *Announcement*, p. 15.
9. Syracuse University, New York, School of Library Studies, 1979–1980 *Bulletin*, p. 16.
10. Unpublished survey conducted by Information Alternative, 1980.
11. Ibid.
12. Ibid.
13. Kent State University, School of Library Science, Summer 1980 *Bulletin*, p. 2.
14. Womanschool, New York City, *Bulletin* 1980, p. 2.
15. International Center of Photography, *Lectures, Workshops and Courses*, p. 9.

CHAPTER EIGHT

NETWORKING

What is networking?

Very simply, networking is the cultivation of contacts for a purpose—for moral support, to gain information, for advice, or for referrals and recommendations.

Networking is calling up a commercial artist you met at an art gallery opening party to ask for a recommendation of a printer to do your brochure. It is having lunch with another small business owner and discussing new ways of advertising. It is sending a short note to an old college roommate to congratulate him or her on promotion to vice president of a bank.

On the surface, networking sounds manipulative and selfish. Deliberately being friendly to another person for your own gain *is* manipulative and selfish, but that is not networking. Everyone who belongs to a network benefits. You never know when you will repay a favor received from someone else.

For example, that artist you met at a cocktail party may someday ask you for advice on collecting rare art books. The small business owner you had lunch with might seek your advice on records management. The old college roommate turned bank vice president may have a relative or friend who is interested in starting a fee-based information service.

Networking can be as informal or as formal as you want it to be. You do not need to organize a group of people and call it a network to be networking. In fact, you are probably already networking, but you do not call it such. If you belong to at least one club, organization, or association, you are already plugged into a network. If you have ever stopped a person at a convention and said, "Your badge says Detroit. I'm from Detroit, too," you are already networking.

Businessmen have used networking for years to "get ahead," but it is a fairly new idea for most women, and with good reason. Until recently, most women were not seriously involved in the work force and there was no reason to develop a network if there was no chance of getting ahead. Work for most women was something to do until marriage, or later, when the kids were grown; or "something to fall back on" in case "something happened" to a husband. Women did not generally engage in sports activities so there was no reason to join a country club or tennis club, nor was there a possibility of being accepted into a sports club because most excluded women or allowed only members' wives to join.

But that was then and this is now. Today, if you own and operate a fee-based information service, you will need to know as much about using networks as you can, and fortunately there are many networks now open to you.

YOUR PERSONAL NETWORK

The easiest network to join is your own personal network of people you already know. There are no membership dues involved and no special requirements. Your own personal network is already in motion.

Your informal network is probably bigger than you think, so do not underestimate it. If you were asked to rattle off the names of 25 people you know, you might have a hard time recalling more than a dozen or so names on the spot, but given the right set of circumstances and enough time, you would probably be able to come up with many more than 25.

So, why not give yourself the right set of circumstances and enough time? Set aside an afternoon or evening and begin work on compiling your personal network file. A good place to start would be your client file. Remember when you went through the names of people you know who might be potential clients? Go back over those names and include them in your network file.

Creating a network file need not be as formal as creating a client file, but some type of written record is helpful. Having a file box full of cards, or a rolodex, or a file of business cards is handier than trying to recall names and phone numbers when you need to find someone in a hurry.

Now go back and think of all the people you did not include in your client file and add those names to your network file, including the names of people you went to school with, former co-workers, friends, friends of friends, and relatives. (Actually, all those names should be in your client file, too.)

Think about those people and their areas of expertise and how they might help you. Your neighbor's daughter works for a computer manufacturer. Could she advise you on the purchase of computers for your company? Could she furnish you with the name of someone at her company who could talk to you? Your nephew works in the payroll department of a small firm. Could he tell you anything about payroll that might apply to your company? Could he give you the name of a company that prints customized business forms?

Do not worry about "using" family or friends. If you approach them in the right way and end with an offer to return a favor, most people will be happy to share their knowledge with you.

Next, think of the types of people you would like to meet. Do you wish to meet other owners/operators of fee-based information services? Other small business owners? Other executives?

To help you decide whom you would like to meet, think about who you are and where you are headed in business. As the owner/operator of a fee-based information service, you are also:

An information professional
A business owner
A small businessperson
A man or a woman
A consultant
A librarian
A writer
An editor
A college graduate
A professional similar to doctor, lawyer
An executive
Self-employed
A troubleshooter

A teacher
A taxpayer
An indexer
A cataloger
An expert
A lecturer
A publisher
A researcher
A librarian
A personnel consultant
A buyer
A public relations expert

You will want to meet with others who share the same problems you do, although they may not necessarily work in the information field.

Where you are going depends on your own set of goals and future plans for your company. Perhaps you are self-employed, but have hopes of managing a large fee-based information service. You would like to meet other managers. Maybe you are satisfied being self-employed, but you would like to meet others in the health care field because you are gaining expertise in this area and plan to become a specialist within the next few years.

Where can you meet people to add to your own personal network? Finding out about people to add to your informal network will follow the same routine as locating experts or clients for your business. Thumb through directories, cull names from literature, ask other people for their recommendations.

Once you have the name of a person plus some background information, all you have to do is call and invite him or her to lunch. It is easier than it sounds. Although there is some risk involved (the person could say no), you have much more to lose by not calling.

If you are hesitant about calling someone, ask a friend to help you rehearse your speech. You will play you and your friend can play the person you are inviting to lunch. First, you will invite a friendly, agreeable person to lunch, next a noncommunicative person, then a downright hostile person. The person you call is bound to be one of the three types, and you will be prepared to deal with any one of them.

Why would anyone want to have lunch with a total stranger? Why not? If you establish yourself as someone equally important as the person you are calling, you will offer as much as you receive. The person at the other end of the line may welcome a chance to speak with someone in a fascinating profession. He or she may be pleased at being called on for advice from another expert.

When you place your call, be sure to make it clear that you are not job hunting and that you are not trying to sell your services. Quickly establish yourself and the matter you would like to discuss. For example: "Hello, this is Mary Jones of Jones and Associates, a health care information service. I'm interested in learning more about geriatrics and I thought, since you are the author of *Geriatrics in the 1980s*, we might get together to discuss some of the issues you raised in your book. Would you have time next week to meet for lunch?"

These sentences establish you as an expert in your field, tell her you know how important she is (you read her book, didn't you?), set forth a specific issue, and compel her to respond to your lunch invitation. This speech may sound unnatural, but it is an effective way of communicating. A more natural but ineffective opening would be: "Hi, this is Mary Jones. I'd like to learn about geriatrics. Would you like to have lunch?" This leaves the person to wonder who Mary Jones is (a college student doing a paper, a job hunter?) and why she was unlucky enough to be picked by Mary for a lunch date. If she is a busy person, she will not bother to find out who Mary is or why she called. She will simply decline and breathe a sigh of relief.

What happens if you have lunch with someone and it turns out that you do not get along very well? Just chalk it up to experience. Networking is a human process, not a mechanical one. Just as you do not like everyone else in this world, you may not like some of the people you meet through networking. You have lost nothing, and if you feel you do not want to pursue a relationship, simply drop the person from your informal network.

JOINING LOCAL NETWORKS

Joining local clubs, organizations, and associations is another method of meeting new people to add to your own personal network. To find a network, check your local Yellow Pages under the headings "Associations," "Clubs," "Fraternal Organizations," and "Labor Organizations." Ask acquaintances for the names of organizations they belong to and watch for announcements of meetings in the local press.

If you do not already have a friend in the group who can tell you its purpose and goals, request descriptive literature about the organization so that you can determine whether it is worth your time to attend a meeting.

Once you have joined an organization, you can use your membership as clout when you invite another member to lunch. Who could turn down a fellow member of the same club?

STARTING A LOCAL NETWORK

But what if there are no appropriate organizations in your area? What if you live in a rural or suburban area far away from the resources of a large city?

Start your own group! Forming a network is easier than you think. Start by inviting two or three women (or men) interested in networking and their friends to meet for lunch. Choose a restaurant with reasonably priced food, but—more important—with a separate area for your meetings. To simplify ordering, hold choices to two or three entrées and place the order in advance. Plan to hold meetings at the same place, at the same time, say the first and third Tuesdays of each month, and stick to the schedule.

At the first meeting explain the purpose of the network, have each member introduce himself or herself, and decide on membership requirements if any. You will want to keep the first meeting simple to allow for any snags including problems with service, late arrivals, and initial reserve.

In the beginning you will have to do most of the work until you are able to delegate tasks to other regular members, so keep things simple.

The first few meetings should be devoted to getting to know the other members and determining the group's direction. While the group is small, each member can tell what he or she hopes to get out of being a part of the group.

After the group has met a few times, a more ambitious agenda can be planned to include invited speakers or a vital-questions panel to address issues of importance to the group.

For further details on starting a network, see *Networking: A Great New Way for Women to Get Ahead,* by Mary-Scott Welch (Warner Books, 1980), or *Is Networking for You? A Working Woman's Alternative to the Old Boy System,* by Barbara B. Stern (Prentice-Hall, 1981).

NATIONAL BUSINESS ORGANIZATIONS

Membership in national organizations is expensive. In a survey conducted by Information Alternative of 75 national library, business, and information organizations, basic membership dues ranged from a low of $15 per year to $250 and upward per year.[1] At these prices, joining more than one or two organizations can put a dent in the budget of a fledgling business.

So why join a national organization whose headquarters is located in a city hundreds of miles away from your office? What can you expect to gain by joining a national business organization? Here are some benefits to consider when evaluating an organization.

Annual convention. What is the cost of attending the group's convention, including transportation, meals, hotel, and registration fee? What can a convention offer you in terms of continuing education, networking with other members, and current awareness? If your only interest in the group is the annual convention, can you attend as a nonmember for a slightly higher registration fee and save the cost of membership? Is the convention always held in the same city (lucky for you if this happens to be your hometown) or does the site rotate in various part of the country, giving all members an opportunity to attend?

Regional meetings. In addition to the annual convention, does the group hold regular monthly, weekly, or quarterly meetings in your region of the country? Will you be able to attend a local meeting if the meeting site is more than a few miles away? The cost of transportation to and from meetings, plus meals eaten in restaurants in connection with meetings, can add up over a year.

Special divisions. What special areas of concern are addressed by the group's special-interest divisions? Are these your areas of concern as well? What is the cost of joining a special division?

Directory. Does the group publish a well-organized, comprehensive directory? (If it does not, the group can become a client and the organization of a directory could be your next job.) A directory can link you with other members throughout the country.

Newsletter. Does the organization's newsletter keep you informed of current events in the world of business, report successes of other members' businesses whose methods can be applied to your firm, summarize meetings you are unable to attend, and provide resource lists for business owners?

Other publications. Handbooks, guidebooks, sample forms, how-to's, and other publications are often published by business organizations and made available to members at discount prices.

Insurance. Group policies are available through several national business organizations at lower rates than individual policies.

Credit union. As a member of a large, national organization you may be eligible to join a credit union.

Educational programs. In addition to annual conventions, check to see what the organization has to offer in the way of seminars in your area and printed educational tools.

Job bank. Job banks are not to be overlooked as a source of clients.

Following is a short resource list of some of the national business organizations that might be of special interest to women. (This list is not meant as an endorsement of any group.)

American Business Women's Association, Box 8728, Kansas City, MO 64114. ABWA is "dedicated to the professional, educational, social and cultural advancement of business women."[2] It offers its 100,000 members hotel discounts, insurance, and a free publication, "Women in Business," and holds regional meetings and an annual convention.

American Society of Professional and Executive Women, 1511 Walnut St., Philadelphia, PA 19102. "Provides a unique support system that backs your special interests."[3] Members receive hotel discounts, insurance, free periodicals, and discounts on publications. Financial and business seminars are held throughout the country.

International Organization of Women Executives, 1800 N. 78 Court, Elmwood Park, IL 60635. IOWE members receive a newsletter, insurance, credit union application, access to job bank, and directory. The group holds an annual convention and conducts frequent seminars.

National Association of Women Business Owners, 2000 P St. N.W., Washington, DC 20036. "A primary need of any business owner is contacts, others in the business community with whom you share mutual interests of ownership, important business referrals and expertise. The National Association of Women Business Owners was formed by enlightened women entrepreneurs to communicate and share experiences and talents with others in ownership or management positions, and to use their collective influence to broaden opportunities for women.[4] NAWBO membership services include a monthly newsletter, listing in a national index of women-owned businesses, and other publications. The group sponsors 12 regional meetings a year and an annual convention.

National Small Business Association, NSB Building, 1604 K Street N.W., Washington, DC 20006. NSB is the oldest organization in the United States representing small business. The group does not hold meetings or sponsor a convention, but works in Congress for passage of laws favorable to small business. Members receive a newsletter, notification of government procurement contracts, and a low-cost insurance program.

LIBRARY AND INFORMATION ORGANIZATIONS

In determining which library and information organizations will be of value to you and your business, use the same criteria as for business organizations. It may also interest you to know which organizations other owners/operators of fee-based information services belong to. Respondents to a survey of 75 fee-based information services cited membership in the following library and information organizations:[5]

American Library Association—16
American Society for Information Science—17

American Society of Indexers—3
Canadian Library Association—10
Information Industry Association—10
Special Libraries Association—24

Survey respondents also mentioned membership in state or province library associations (12), local or national business associations (15), specialized library associations (10), and other associations of a special nature (12).

Here are some details about several library and information organizations that may be of interest:

American Library Association (ALA), 50 E. Huron St., Chicago, IL 60611. Members receive publications; annual convention and regional meetings are held.

American Society for Information Science (ASIS), 1010 16 St. N.W., Washington, DC 20036. "ASIS is dedicated to the improvement of the information-transfer process through research, development, application and education. It is concerned with the generation, collection, organization, interpretation, storage, retrieval, dissemination, transformation, and use of information, with particular emphasis on the applications of modern technologies in these areas.[6] Membership benefits include publications, placement service, group insurance, and directory. The group holds an annual convention and regional meetings.

American Society of Indexers (ASI), 235 Park Ave. S., New York, NY 10003. Members receive a newsletter and other publications including "Register of Indexers." There are two meetings per year.

Associated Information Managers (AIM), 316 Pennsylvania Ave. S.E., Suite 502, Washington, DC 20003. "AIM offers a management perspective and enables information managers to learn from peers, through case studies and through formal educational programs."[7] AIM holds an annual meeting and sponsors regional seminars and workshops. Members receive a newsletter, a membership directory, a document alert system, and other publications.

Information Industry Association (IIA), 316 Pennsylvania Ave. S.E., Suite 502, Washington, D.C. 20003. Membership benefits include a newsletter, special reports, a directory, legislative representation. IIA holds an annual meeting and exhibit.

Special Libraries Association (SLA), 235 Park Ave. S., New York, NY 10003. Members receive a division newsletter or bulletin, other publications, job-bank services, consulting service, and continuing education courses. Annual conference and regional meetings are held.

Women Library Workers, Box 9052, Berkeley, CA 94709. Members receive a periodical and moral support from active local chapters. There are regional meetings and a national conference.

DOS AND DON'TS FOR NETWORKING WITH OTHER OWNERS/OPERATORS

1. Do not be afraid to network with fellow information brokers, freelance librarians, or others in your area for fear they will steal your ideas or learn about "inside" information you would rather not reveal. They may be competitors, but also your allies. Above all others, another information broker understands the problems and difficulties unique to this business. You can both gain from an exchange of ideas without revealing trade secrets. If there are no other fee-based information services in your area, networking via mail or phone can help you feel less isolated from the mainstream.

2. Do repay a favor before you are asked to. If another person has spent time with you over the phone or during a lunch hour, you owe that person a favor. If there is nothing you can do right away, at least send a thank-you letter extending an offer to help in whatever way you can in the future.

3. Do not gossip to a freelance librarian, information broker, or other person about someone else in the field. Gossip serves no purpose in a business relationship.

4. Do invite a fellow freelance librarian, information broker, or other person to join your personal network or organization if you think he or she will benefit from joining.

5. Do not call another owner/operator of a fee-based information service and say, "I'm thinking about going into the business. How do you do it?" You would be surprised at some of the letters and phone calls received at established fee-based information services. I have been asked to provide callers with sample products, compile comprehensive bibliographies, and supply clients to services not yet in existence.

6. Do your homework before you place a call or write a letter to a fee-based information service asking for information or advice. Use your information-gathering skills to do your background research on fee-based information services and small businesses. Use your interviewing skills to formulate specific, answerable questions.

BASIC QUESTIONS AND ANSWERS

Q. What is networking?

A. Cultivating contacts for advice, information, or referrals and recommendations.

Q. What is a personal network file?

A. A written record of names and numbers of people you know, went to school with, or worked with, as well as relatives and friends of friends.

Q. What is a good way to enlarge your network options?

A. Join local clubs, organizations, and associations.

Q. What are the benefits of joining national business organizations?

A. Continuing contacts from annual conventions or regional meetings; organization directories, which can give you a link to other members; newsletters and other publications of the organizations; insurance; credit unions; and educational programs.

NOTES

1. Unpublished survey conducted by Information Alternative, 1979.
2. American Business Women's Association, letter to prospective members.
3. American Society of Professional and Executive Women, letter to prospective members.
4. National Association of Women Business Owners, promotional brochure.
5. "Where Are We Now?" *Journal of Fee-Based Information Services* 2, no. 1 (January/February 1980): 3.
6. American Society for Information Science, promotional brochure.
7. Associated Information Managers, brochure.

IF I HAD
IT ALL
TO
DO AGAIN

One of the best things about not being "the first" to do something
is that you can gain from the experience and trial and error of those
who traveled the road before you. In this chapter, information
brokers answer some questions concerned with the past, and their
answers should prove helpful to those who are about to enter this
challenging field.*

Q. If you were establishing a fee-based information service within
   a library today, what would you do differently?

A. *(Jean Piety, Facts For a Fee, Cleveland Public Library)* I don't
   think I'd have done anything differently. We had a smooth start
   and have enjoyed even growth over the years.

Q. If you were starting a fee-based information service today,
   what would you do differently?

A. *(Matthew Lesko, Washington Researchers)* I would charge
   more than I did in the beginning. In retrospect I feel that I
   underpriced my services. Along these lines, I would have
   raised my prices instead of hiring people to handle an increased workload.

---

*Replies to questions were obtained by the author via telephone con-
versations with those named, and the information is used with permission.

Q. What advice would you give to someone starting a fee-based information service within a university?

A. *(Tina Byrne, Co-Director, Regional Information and Communication Exchange at Rice University)* Establishing and running such a service is an expensive proposition, which requires close monitoring both through expenses and types (and success) of services rendered. Above all, your perception must include looking at your services as a business.

Q. What advice would you give to anybody going into this business?

A. *(Tim Knier, Director, Knier Associates)* I'd recommend that the person considering the field have a background in computers or become familiar with computers by delving into the literature. As law book appraisers we use word-processing equipment to keep our clients' inventories and our own inventory in order. Knowledge of computers is also necessary for doing on-line searches.

Q. If you were starting today what would you do differently?

A. *(Tim Knier, Director, Knier Associates)* I don't think I'd do anything differently.

Q. What advice would you give a person in a private or corporate fee-based information service?

A. *(Gary Bratton, Vice President, Infosource, Inc.,* a subsidiary of Allegheny Ludlum Industries) Never turn down a job because you're busy or because it's out of your realm of expertise. It's better to subcontract a job to another broker than to refuse a client. The client need never know who worked on the job.

Q. How would you advise someone who wanted to start a fee-based information service within a corporation?

A. *(Melinda Scott, Senior Consultant and Director of Management Research Group, Peat, Marwick, Mitchell and Co.)* Attach yourself to the main pipeline, get involved in planning, offer to sit in on meetings, and low-key sell your ideas all the time.

Q. As an economist, how would you advise persons who want to start fee-based information services?

A. *(Marc Porat, information economist, author and producer of the film* The Information Society*)* Examine the growth of the temporary services industry, which I see as a parallel industry, to see how it developed and became a successful alternative. Also, take a look at what's happening in the management consultant field—how it is making progress, how management consultants build a clientele.

Q. What advice would you give to a person starting a fee-based information service:

A. *(Matthew Lesko, Washington Researchers)* Don't worry about anything except getting clients!

Don't worry about accountants or getting a lawyer. Don't worry about gaining prestige. All your energies should be directed toward getting customers. Don't waste any of your time doing anything other than getting customers.

I've had two other businesses before this, plus seven years of business schooling. I ran the other businesses by the book, but they folded because I spent so much energy on the things you're supposed to do.

Wait until you're successful to worry about all those things you're supposed to do in the business world. In the beginning don't worry about anything else because all you need to open your business is a business card and stationery.

Don't hire other people unless you have too much money! Always raise your prices first before you hire somebody else. You can eliminate some of your work and earn more money by increasing your prices, and then after you've raised your prices it's easier to hire somebody if needed.

In this kind of business if you're bootstrapping, living from hand to mouth, you get too busy, then you hire somebody else and forget about the economics of this business. I think there are diseconomies of scale in growth in this business. Growth does not necessarily mean a larger profit. When you're smaller you can really do things cheaper. It's really more expensive to be larger, and people think it's the other way around.

Stretch your imagination as much as you can in the area of marketing. Give away as much as you can. For example, the newsletter we publish was at one time free.

If prospective clients call me, I let them pick my brains for free. I won't research for free, but I'll show them how smart I am for free!

You have nothing to lose when starting a business by giving things away for free because you have nowhere to go but up.

You can give away a service if you don't have a product. You can offer to answer the first question for free off the top of your head or give away a source of information. This generates excitement and need and that's a way to get business.

If you've got nothing better to do, it's better to work for free than not to work at all.

Create a product to give away. If I were in a regional area, I'd put together a product identifying the ten best information sources in the area, print it up, and give it out as a free handout. Then I'd send a press release and that would generate more publicity than thousands of dollars worth of advertising could buy.

Identify who you're appealing to and what your clients' needs are. Then give away what clients want, in a small way, and they'll return to you for the details. Who else would they go to?

For example, if you live in a high-technology area, write a brief report identifying areas of growth for high technology and make it available to clients, the general public, and the press. When the press writes this up, anybody needing more details will have to ask you.

There is no magic to being successful. In the beginning you must zero in on what's really important and believe there's no way to do it except your way. The only way people can add any magic is to do it their way and not Washington Researchers' way or anybody else's way. Creating something you believe in is the best way you become successful.

Q. What would you do differently if you had an opportunity to start over?

A. *(Barbara Whyte Felicetti, Director, Info/motion)* When I began my business five years ago, after graduating from library school, I spent a great deal of time taking additional library courses. These provided me with a very friendly, familiar turf to return to, which helped me feel less isolated and kept me going. Of course, these additional courses also helped me add to my repertoire of library skills.

However, if I were going to do it again, instead of taking additional library school courses I would take business courses at the graduate level. I still feel at a distinct disadvantage in not having a business background. Without business courses I've had to learn how to run a business by the seat of my pants.

Looking back at a different aspect, much sooner than I did, I would have hired another person to work with me. I would have hired someone with whom I could have shared both the problems and joys of running the business and doing projects. The people whom I ultimately found who serve that role have made what could be very lonely, more adventurous and more fun. Working alone is the hardest part for me. The isolation of this business is unbelievable. I enjoy team effort and I enjoy having someone to talk to about the business.

I have an extremely helpful husband who took the time to sit down with me and help me chart my business's progress. I probably wouldn't have done this on my own. Not realizing I was successful would have killed my enthusiasm and I probably wouldn't still be in the business.

Q. What advice would you give to someone starting in this business?

A. *(Barbara Whyte Felicetti, Director, Info/motion)* Don't be afraid of mistakes. Appreciate risks instead of fearing them. Prepare yourself for risks and learn from them because every mistake is as important as every success in the learning process.

I learn as much from proposals that don't fly as I do from proposals that work. When something doesn't work, I try to find out why. And you must ask for feedback because people don't offer it on their own.

Also, learn to recognize isolation for what it is instead of having a free-floating feeling that something is wrong. When you're in a pioneering area, when people perceive you as a threat, and many people will, you will feel isolated from others.

Although I'm in a rural area and physically isolated, this type of isolation can happen in a large city as well.

Q. If you were starting over what would you change?

A. *(Ellen Boughn Henderson, After-Image, Inc., Los Angeles)* I would never start a filing system that wasn't computer compatible—the system I work with isn't.

I started my business in 1976 and I started with no money—literally. I came to the field from a background in zoology and educational film writing. I saw a need in Los Angeles for a photo research company and when I started there were none. I began by emptying my recipe file box and filling it with index cards. I went around to photographers and inventoried and indexed their photos. I now have a collection of over 100,000 35mm slides. It's very difficult to keep track of a collection this size, and I'm trying to develop a computerized system that will work as a clerical aide rather than an information retriever. In a visual medium it makes very little sense to use an information retrieval system that would call up terms like islands or manufacturing if you wanted a picture of a salt mine in the Caribbean because visual images vary. I need a system that would read a number on a slide, but working with such a small surface—a 35mm slide is only 2 by 2—prevents most computer systems from working.

Q. What would you do differently if you were starting over?

A. *(Ty Webb, Info Webb, a fee-based information service in Kansas City, Missouri)* Not much! I planned to build my business while my daughter was growing up and work around her schedule when she entered school. Despite the addition of another child, I've managed to stay right on schedule. I even searched while I was in labor and I take my son with me on some jobs.

Q. How would you advise someone starting a fee-based information service now?

A. *(Ty Webb, Info Webb)* Know your community and your community's information needs. Strive to become well known in your local community. This is, for now, the most important aspect.

Q. How do you advise incoming students who want to open fee-based information services?

A. *(Robert Taylor, Dean, Syracuse University School of Information Studies)* This would depend on whether the student wanted to start an independent brokering company or go to work for a large brokering company. I would advise, in any case, that a student take a number of basic information courses. Beyond this I would suggest a marketing course, taken either through the business school or here at the library school (we offer frequent seminars in marketing). A good background in marketing is needed both from the standpoint of marketing the service and marketing him- or herself. Also required is a knowledge of financial statements and data.

Beyond this it would depend on the student's own interests. All of our program is comprised of electives, and programs are tailored to meet the needs of individual students. We have enough leeway in our program to allow for students to do independent projects where we may not have a course.

In advising students on their choice of courses, we discuss their background and future plans. For example, a student with a paralegal background could do well as a law library consultant.

I suggest that people in rural areas not relocate to cities but stay in their area and seek out as clients small local governments and historical societies and the like. They won't make a great deal of money and it won't be easy, but with political acumen they will be successful.

Last, I would advise a student to believe in one's own capabilities, to have enough capital to last one year and plenty of chutzpah!

Q. What would you do differently if you were to start over tomorrow?

A. *(Judith Mahrer, Library Services,* law library consultancy in Denver, Colorado) I think our prices were too low when we started. I would have learned more about pricing. Also, I would have prepared myself to deal with what turned out to be my biggest headaches—personnel management and administration.

Q. How would you advise someone going into the business today?

A. *(Judith Mahrer, Library Services)* I think people should think very carefully—do they want to be a one-person operation and be totally in control of their own lives, or do they want to administer a business?

Q. What is the one thing you would tell library school students who plan to open their own companies?

A. *(Kelly Warnken, Owner/Director, Information Alternative,* speaking at the "So You Want to Be an Information Broker?" seminar, May 1981) If your school doesn't offer a course in information brokering, take an independent study in brokering. But don't do a paper on the history and future of information brokering; don't send out a survey to 100 information brokering companies asking them how they started, who their clients are, and what they do; this has been done many times before and won't be of much use to you when you start your business. Instead, do a market study of your area, concentrate on yourself and your business rather than surveying the field in general. Use the time you have in library school to prepare yourself as best you can for opening day. Since you won't get paid for the many hours you put into doing background research, you might as well at least earn a grade for your troubles!

THE
FUTURE

What is the future of the fee-based information industry? What can a new information broker expect? For a look at the future, information brokers gave their answers to a number of questions concerned with what is on the horizon for the industry.*

Q. Do you see a future for fee-based information services in public libraries?

A. *(Jean Piety, Facts For a Fee, Cleveland Public Library)* Yes. More and more libraries are beginning to think about starting fee-based information services. So many, in fact, that we've had to develop a set of guidelines to send to librarians who write to us for advice.

Q. Do you think the future of the fee-based information services industry lies in large companies or small services?

A. *(Matthew Lesko, Washington Researchers)* There is a dynamite future for librarians who want to work out of their homes. When you get to be large, you get an overhead that forces you to charge $50–$75 per hour. I don't think clients are willing to accept the high fees charged by large information brokerage firms, which are asked out of necessity to cover a large over-

*Replies to questions were obtained by the author via telephone conversations with those named, and the information is used with permission.

head. People who work out of their homes can work for a lot less and work a lot better. When you're small you control the quality of the work you offer because you do the work yourself. When you have a large staff the quality of work varies with the person assigned to the job on that particular day. There is a large need and there will continue to be a need for fee-based information services.

Q. Do you think fee-based information service is a growing industry?

A. *(Gary Bratton, Vice President, Infosource, Inc.,* a subsidiary of Allegheny Ludlum Industries) This is definitely a growing field, but unfortunately few library schools are addressing the training needs of people who plan to work in the field.

Q. Do you think fee-based information services within corporations will continue to grow?

A. *(Melinda Scott, Senior Consultant and Director of Management Research Group, Peat, Marwick, Mitchell and Co.)* Yes. As the information-conscious begin to graduate from universities and enter the business world, there continues to be a gradual revolution toward better information and better use of information in companies. Fee-based information services within corporations are a part of this gradual revolution in the business world.

Q. What do you see as the future of your company?

A. *(Tim Knier, Director, Knier Associates)* We started out as a management consultant firm for law libraries and have expanded into publishing, loose-leaf filing services, and appraising law books. We plan to develop a series of audiovisual training guides and to form a national network of law book appraisers. Our goal is to have so much business we'll have to turn people away!

Q. What do you see as the future of the fee-based information services industry?

A. *(Marc Porat, information economist, author and producer of the film* The Information Society*)* This is definitely a growth business. I believe there will be an ad hoc development of the business for the next few years until a national company comes into being.

Libraries (public) are definitely the place for fee-based information services because they serve the needs of the middle class and they can better serve these needs by providing better services through fee-based services.

Q. What do you see as the future of fee-based information services in Canada?

A. *(SIS, Ltd.)* The need for a total information management service is evident to us as more and more companies in Canada experience growth problems, which in turn become information management problems. In the future there will be an even greater emphasis on information management.

Q. What do you see as the future of your service?

A. *(Tina Byrne, Co-Director, Regional Information and Communication Exchange at Rice University)* Originally we operated as a network consortium and our primary function was retrieval of in-house material. We've evolved naturally with the information climate and for the past four years have been dynamic in meeting the information needs of our business community. Our primary goal is to provide the best and most prompt service required to meet our clients' various information needs. We are constantly exploring and soliciting suggestions and resources and products to be better able to meet our clients' requirements in the future.

Q. What do you see as the future of fee-based information services in England?

A. *(Nigel Oxbrow, Director, London Researchers)* The outlook is excellent because it's a growing industry. I'd say we're about five years behind the States, though, so come back and see me in five years and I'll tell you how things are then!

Q. Looking down the road five or ten years from now, what issues could impact detrimentally on the information business —particularly on information brokers?

A. *(Andrew Garvin, FIND/SVP)* First of all, I think there will always be a market for freelance research or contract-on-demand research. I would say there are a number of possible pitfalls ahead, however. One is the tendency of companies, especially large companies, to build their own internal resources. We at FIND consider the most significant competition we have to be a company's internal resources. Second, there is the issue of computer data bases. In brokering data bases, the question immediately arises that if everyone ultimately has a terminal at his or her desk, who needs a broker? We feel that if that is going to come about (and we doubt it), it will be very far away. In the meantime we find that people who are aware of data bases, even if they have their own terminals, seek assistance from us because it's extremely difficult to follow all of the data bases, be trained on all of them, and to know which to search for what. We have calculated that before we answer a single question, it probably costs us $50,000 a year to maintain all our equipment and to have an appropriate number of people trained on the data bases to do cost-effective searching.

In computer searching, it depends on the pricing strategy, but in some cases, I know people sell individual computer searches for $150, $200, or $250, even though computer searches can be done for a lot less. So if a broker is selling volume computer searches that may be another industry in and of itself.

I think these are some problems to which more attention might be given in the future.

Q. What do you see as the future of your company?

A. *(Barbara Whyte Felicetti, Director, Info/motion)* What we will continue to do is to put out a high quality product. That's the most important thing that we do. In the future I would envision that we would service multinational clients and that we would have full telecommunications capabilities, including capabilities of doing our own searching and having word-processing equipment. The size organization I would hope to have in the future is, in addition to myself, five full-time professionals and eight full-time support staff members.

Q. Do you think this is a growing field?

A. *(Richard S. Halsey, Dean, State University of New York at Albany School of Library and Information Science)* When people go into library school they are faced with the traditional kinds of librarianship and think in terms of school libraries, public libraries, and special libraries. When you begin to discuss the employment possibilities and examine a shrinking job market for traditionally trained librarians, you realize the potential of this field.

Looking at our own graduates, over 30 percent now work in nontraditional settings using information.

Industry is beginning to realize it's more cost-effective to bring in an information broker or information consultant than to get stuck with someone who will be attached permanently to the organization.

Data processing is also beginning to realize the value of having an information consultant working in tandem with the data processor because of the expertise an information consultant can bring to the job.

I believe fee-based information services belong in public libraries because certain kinds of information services can be offered only on a fee basis. I think the city fathers, the people who give money to public libraries, would respect fee-based services offered within libraries.

In the future information brokers will help others cope with the overload of underutilized, sloppily and chaotically organized information, which is now not being used to capacity. People are frustrated and become stuck when searching for information. They prefer to work with one person such as an information broker than to have to deal with a bureaucracy such as a library.

If I were not already dean of a library school, I'd be thinking of forming a small group of four or five people that would be available as consultants to many libraries!

Q. What do you see happening in the area of visual information services in the near future?

A. *(Ellen Boughn Henderson, After-Image, Inc., Los Angeles, a visual research company)* Computers in the near future will have the capability to operate as a visual as well as printed information retrieval service. Photographers will be able to transmit their photographs through computer directly to the user—the ad agency, book publisher, film producer—to use as is in an ad or a book or to hang on the walls of a movie set.

One of two things will happen. Either I will be put out of business by this technological advancement because there will be no need for photo research services if photographers can supply their own photographs directly to clients, or my function will change and I'll act as a clearinghouse for photographers who are unable to put their own work on-line because of lack of expertise or because of the cost involved in doing this.

Q. What will affect fee-based information services in the near future?

A. (*Ty Webb, Info Webb,* a fee-based information service in Kansas City, Missouri) Ours is an electronic cottage industry. We provide on-line searching services and other supplementary library services. I'm beginning to notice that computerization and automation are entering into every aspect of my business.

Currently I have some clients I've never seen. We communicate over the phone, the request is submitted over the phone, the search is run via our computer terminal, and the results of the search are sent directly to the client. I think we'll see more and more of that in the future.

Within the next ten years, selling information as a product will become easier. The fact that needs can be met with a consumer product—information—will be readily accepted. Businesses will realize the availability of information services, their importance, and how much they are needed.

Q. What do you see in the future for fee-based information services?

A. (*Robert Taylor, Dean, Syracuse University School of Information Studies*) I rather think there is a good future. I wish public libraries would wake up to this fact! I think public libraries should become warehouses and rent offices to all kinds of independents including lawyers and information brokers who use the collections. Or they should establish and concentrate on marketing their own in-house fee-based information services.

Q. What are your own goals for the future?

A. *(Judith Mahrer, Library Services,* a law library consultancy in Denver, Colorado) I'd like to get Denver freelancers together to meet, cooperate, and share with each other. I feel everyone would benefit from knowing each other's specialties. I refer to other freelancers all the time and I'm currently working on a large joint project with another freelancer. I'd also like to publish a directory of alternative librarians in Denver similar to the one in Toronto.

We're presently heavily dependent on one service we offer—loose-leaf filing—and it's never good to rely on a single service. This is why I'd like to diversify into other areas such as Westlaw searches and legal memoranda file design.

I'm expanding geographically as well. The western slope of Colorado, the area outside of the metropolitan Denver area, is very badly served in terms of any legal materials, and we are seeking new clients in this area.

Q. What do you see as the future of fee-based information services?

A. *(Kelly Warnken, Owner/Director, Information Alternative)* In the next few years large corporations will enter the fee-based information services industry in greater numbers. They will offer high-priced, impersonal, mediocre services primarily to the business community. Their positive contribution to the industry will be in raising the public's consciousness of fee-based information services. This will in turn make it easier for the small, privately owned company and the single-person company to be successful at offering reasonably priced, personal, high-quality services to businesses, professionals, and nonprofit organizations.

ANNOTATED BIBLIOGRAPHY

by S. C. van der Valk

This annotated bibliography of the development of fee-based information brokers in North America is divided according to subject headings, with entries dealing with Canada preceding American articles. Listings under each country are alphabetical by author. Following the main bibliography are entries that involve such educational aspects as workshops and courses and items of interest in other countries.

Research for compiling this bibliography entailed a literature review of material on commercial fee-based information services. The professional library indexes consulted were *Library Literature* and *Library and Information Science Abstracts*, 1960 to 1980, which led to articles in other journals and books.

BIBLIOGRAPHIES

CANADIAN

Klement, S. "Selected Annotated Bibliography of Articles Relevant to Alternatives in Librarianship." *Canadian Library Journal* 34, no. 2 (April 1977): 137–140. A listing of 41 articles to accompany the proposed course for librarians, which is provided in the same issue.

AMERICAN

Davis, M. W. "A Quick Guide to Free Lance Librarianship." *Wilson Library Bulletin* 49, no. 6 (February 1975): 445. A listing of 21 articles.

HISTORICAL BACKGROUND

CANADIAN

Mauerhoff, G. R. "An Information Industry for Canada." *Business Quarterly* 42, no. 2 (September 1977): 35–41. Discusses what conditions in Canadian society will allow for the development of information managers and brokers.

AMERICAN

De Gennaro, R. "Pay Libraries and User Charges." *Library Journal* 100, no. 4 (February 15, 1975): 363–367. Discusses the issue of user charges and whether there is a need for information brokers.

Freeman, J. E., and Katz, R. M. "Information Marketing." In *Annual Review of Information Science and Technology,* ed. by M. E. Williams, vol. 13, pp. 37–60. White Plains, N.Y.: Knowledge Industry Pubs. Inc., 1978. Good general discussion of the factors involved in allowing for the growth of information brokers and their services.

Gaffner, H. B. "The Demand for Information-on-demand." *Bulletin of the American Society for Information Science* 2, no. 7 (February 1976): 39–40. Outlines the stages of development of information brokerage in the United States.

TERMINOLOGY

CANADIAN

Klement, S. "Directory of Alternative Librarians Questionnaire." *Canadian Library Journal* 34, no. 2 (April 1977): 129. List of questions sent to Canadian nontraditional librarians and technicians in an attempt to define their services.

_____. "Introduction—Alternatives in Librarianship." *Canadian Library Journal* 34, no. 2 (April 1977): 77. Personal interpretation of the term *alternative librarian.*

AMERICAN

Albert, T. "The Information Middleman in Energy." *Bulletin of the American Society for Information Science* 2, no. 7 (February 1976): 39. Defines *information broker* and suggests role in handling data.

Albrecht, S., and Redfield, G. "The Traditional Library Setting: Can It Meet the Professional's Needs?" In *What Else You Can Do with a Library Degree,* ed. by Betty-Carol Sellen, pp. 327–339. Syracuse, N.Y.: Gaylord

Professional Pubs., 1980. A questionnaire to determine the motivations and qualifications of those leaving traditional library service.

Boss, R. W. "The Library as an Information Broker." *College and Research Libraries* 40, no. 2 (March 1979): 136–140. Why information brokers sprang up, what they do, and the suggestion that libraries should make themselves aware of these new developments and use them for their own benefit.

Crickman, R. D. "The Emerging Information Professional." *Library Trends* 28, no. 2 (Fall 1979): 311–327. Looks at the role of the information professional.

Deahl, T. F. "Is There an Infotist in the House?" *Bulletin of the American Society for Information Science* 3, no. 2 (December 1976): 17–18. Examines the problem of no clear definition for people who are information professionals.

Dodd, J. B. "Information Brokers." *Special Libraries* 67, no. 5/6 (May/June 1976): 234–250. A comprehensive discussion of brokers in the United States.

Garfield, E. "What Are the Facts (Data) and What Is Information?" In *Essays of an Information Scientist, vol. 2, 1974–1976*, pp. 47–48. Philadelphia, Pa.: I.S.I. Press, 1977. Definitions for data and information.

Hershfield, A. "Information Counselors: A New Profession?" In *Humanization of Knowledge in the Social Sciences—A Symposium*, ed. by P. Atherton, pp. 29–34. Syracuse, N.Y.: Syracuse University, 1972. Discusses phenomena of information deprivation and information overload in American society. Suggests role for information counselors.

"Information Brokers: Who, What, Why, How." *Bulletin of the American Society for Information Science* 2, no. 7 (February 1976): 11–20. Defines *information broker* and summarizes answers to 12 questions sent to 7 organizations (2 Canadian) concerning type of services offered, size of firm, charging methods, resources, role within the library community and the national information network.

Kalba, K. "Libraries in the Information Marketplace." In *Libraries in Post-industrial Society*, ed. by L. Estabrook, pp. 306–320. Phoenix, Ariz.: The Oryx Press, 1977. Examines potential roles of public libraries and information brokers in the future. Defines *information broker* and *infobusiness*.

Lunin, L. F. "The Answer Is Yes: Information Brokers Can Succeed." *Bulletin of the American Society for Information Science* 2, no. 7 (February 1976): 3. Short examination of the status of information brokers in the United States.

Sellen, Betty-Carol, ed. *What Else You Can Do with a Library Degree.* Syracuse, N.Y.: Gaylord Professional Pubs., 1980. A collection of articles by individuals with library science degrees, describing their backgounds, present work, and future prospects. Very good reference book.

Syracuse University. "School of Information Studies 1979–80." *Syracuse University* 4, no. 2 (July 2, 1979): 16. Defines information broker as a freelance information professional who links people to other people and to the information necessary for them to carry on their activities.

INDIVIDUAL COMPANY DESCRIPTIONS

CANADIAN

Campbell, T. "Consulting Services for Business Libraries." *LAA LAA LAA: Newsletter of the Library Association of Alberta.* September 1975, p. 20. Article concerning activities of library consulting firm of P. Schick.

"Canada's First Full-time Library Consultant." *Ontario Library Review* 53, no. 2 (June 1969): 97. Views of Albert Bowron, who began own private business as a library consultant.

Cheda, S. "The Free-lance Alternative in Librarianship—An Interview with Susan Klement." *Canadian Library Journal* 30, no. 5 (September–October 1973): 401–406. Description of types of work and methods of charging by one freelance librarian in Toronto.

Fauman, M. E. "Free-lancing for Law Firm Libraries in Vancouver." *Canadian Association of Law Libraries Newsletter/Bulletin*, October–December 1972, pp. 110–113. Describes library services provided to various law libraries by a freelancer.

Hutton, J. "The Role of the Information Consultant." In *What Else You Can Do with a Library Degree*, ed. by Betty-Carol Sellen, pp. 39–46. Syracuse, N.Y.: Gaylord Professional Pubs., 1980. Concept of information in times of rapid change and the context of information consultants' work. Examples of type of services offered in own company.

Jones, D. J. "Canadian News—At a Price." *Australian Library Journal* 28, no. 12 (July 20, 1979): 180. Account of *Business and Government News*, one service offered by Infomart in Toronto.

"A New Style of Librarian." *The Financial Post Magazine*, November 29, 1980, p. 9. Brief article describing services provided by two Canadian freelance operations.

Schick, P. "Experiences of a Librarian in Business; or Librarians without Libraries." *Manitoba Library Association Bulletin* 7, no. 3 (June 1977): 15–17. The rationale behind the charging for services.

Schlukbier, G. "An Independent Business: Research and Information." In *What Else You Can Do with a Library Degree*, ed. by Betty-Carol Sellen, pp. 23–28. Syracuse, N.Y.: Gaylord Professional Pubs., 1980. Individual's account of leaving traditional library position and beginning own business; steps involved in setting up business.

AMERICAN

Autrey, P. S. "Using Information Skills." In *What Else You Can Do with a Library Degree*, ed. by Betty-Carol Sellen, pp. 10–16. Syracuse, N.Y.: Gaylord Professional Pubs., 1980. Work experiences of past five years of one freelance librarian. Indicates differences between freelancing and working within organizations.

Berger, M. C. "Young Information Professionals." *Bulletin of the American Society for Information Science* 3, no. 2 (December 1976): 11–16. Detailed job profiles of 18 information professionals, including 2 freelancers.

Cohn, E. "Free-lancing after Retirement: The First Year." In *What Else You Can Do with a Library Degree*, ed. by Betty-Carol Sellen, pp. 77–81. Syracuse, N.Y.: Gaylord Professional Pubs., 1980. Experiences of a retired librarian.

Colbert, A. W. "Document Delivery." *Online* 2, no. 2 (April 1978): 77. Sources useful in acquiring material from foreign countries as experienced by the company Information Unlimited.

_____. "Document Delivery." *Online* 2, no. 3 (July 1978): 80–81. Suppliers of government documents used by Information Unlimited.

_____. "Document Delivery." *Online* 2, no. 4 (October 1978): 83–84. Sources used by Information Unlimited to obtain out-of-print books and books published in foreign countries.

_____. "Document Delivery." *Online* 3, no. 1 (January 1979): 61. A list of back-issue periodicals dealers used by Information Unlimited.

_____. "Document Delivery." *Online* 3, no. 2 (April 1979): 70–71. Evaluation of experience with each of the participants in SDC's electronic maildrop system.

_____. "Document Delivery." *Online* 3, no. 3 (July 1979): 66–67. Methods used by Information Unlimited in tracking down authors for requests.

_____. "Document Delivery." *Online* 3, no. 4 (October 1979): 65. Finding a publisher for user requests.

_____. "Document Delivery." *Online* 4, no. 1 (January 1980): 68. The methods used by Information Unlimited to verify and identify conference publications.

_____. "Document Delivery." *Online* 4, no. 2 (April 1980): 70. Sources for Canadian documents as used by Information Unlimited.

_____. "Document Delivery." *Online* 4, no. 3 (July 1980): 66–67. Information concerning organizations that provide seminar papers to a freelance company.

_____. "Document Delivery." *Online* 4, no. 4 (October 1980): 77. Description of three systems set up to provide information retrieval services through on-line ordering as used by Information Unlimited.

Davis, M. W. "The New Information Professional Q's & A's." *NYLA Bulletin* 24 (March 1976): 1, 8. By answering questions of her own, Davis describes her for-profit company, Information Access, and what she feels are the characteristics needed for freelancing.

Doebler, P. "Seek and Ye Shall FIND." *Publishers Weekly* 202, no. 16 (October 16, 1972): 39–42. Description of the question-answering service FIND, in New York City.

Eddison, E. B. "Paid Research Services." *Library Journal* 99, no. 6 (March 15, 1974): 714. Announcing the establishment of an information service in Boston.

"FIND: Information on Demand." *BCLA Reporter* The Newsletter of the British Columbia Library Association 17, no. 6 (June 1974): 19. Brief description of FIND in New York and short background information on Paris company.

Ferguson, P. "Chronicles of an Information Company." *On-Line Review* 1, no. 1 (March 1977): 39–42. The birth and growth of an American West Coast information company is chronicled from its beginning as a part-time partnership to its status five years later as a profitable corporation.

Fiebert, G. "Information for Business." *Information: News and Sources,* January 1975, pp. 29–30. Explanation of organization and services of a company in New York City designed to serve the information needs of business and industry.

Finnigan, G. *The Information Store.* 235 Montgomery St., San Francisco, CA. 94104, 1979. A pamphlet giving prices and resources of photocopy services of this company.

_____. "Nontraditional Information Service." *Special libraries* 67, no. 2 (February 1976): 102–103. Brief description of an independent information service called Information Unlimited in Berkeley, California, which began in 1971.

Finnigan, G., and Rugge, S. "Document Delivery and the Experiences of Information Unlimited." *Online* 2, no. 1 (January 1978): 62–69. This article discusses the problems involved in document delivery and supplies a comprehensive list of addresses for various types of materials.

Goldstein, S. "Information-on-demand: A Brief Summary." *Bulletin of the American Society for Information Science* 2, no. 7 (February 1976): 10. A description of several companies that offer fee-based information services.

Herther, N. K. "Free-lancing: A Personal Experiment." *RQ* 18, no. 2 (Winter 1978): 177–179. Experiences of working as a freelancer for three months and opinions of general aspects involved in going freelance.

Hirsch, A. "Info for Pay Is Better." *Library Journal* 100, no. 8 (April 15, 1975): 702. Reply to article concerning pay libraries and user charges in light of work done by one company, Information Specialists.

Kvamme, J. C. "Free-lancing: A Self Interview." In *What Else You Can Do with a Library Degree,* ed. by Betty-Carol Sellen, pp. 59–67. Syracuse, N.Y.: Gaylord Professional Pubs., 1980. By setting up a list of most commonly asked questions and then answering them, the writer hopes to help others understand what her job encompasses.

Levy, N. E. "Information-on-demand." In *What Else You Can Do with a Library Degree,* ed. by Betty-Carol Sellen, pp. 35–38. Syracuse, N.Y.: Gaylord Professional Pubs., 1980. Provides a good list of types of services offered and a comparative chart of good and bad aspects of freelancing.

Mahrer, J. K., and Helbourn, J. "Law Library Services." In *What Else You Can Do with a Library Degree,* ed. by Betty-Carol Sellen, pp. 47–54. Syracuse, N.Y.: Gaylord Professional Pubs., 1980. Specialization in service to the legal profession on a freelance basis.

Mulligan, G. Finnigan. "Free lancing." *Booklegger* 1, no. 3-4 (March–May 1974): 42–43. Brief description of a fee-based service, Information Unlimited, and speculation on the future of such services in public libraries.

Reavis, J. *Freelance Research Service, Inc.* Library and information specialists. Missouri, TX 77006, 1980. A folder containing a brief guide to services and charges of this particular company.

Rugge, S., and Finnigan, G. "Fee-based Service Misunderstood." *Special Libraries* 69, no. 4 (April 1978): 7a. Comment on article in *Special Libraries,* September 1977, about fee-based service interface; suggests that librarians should see fee-based services as an extension of their own services rather than as threats.

Tomaselli, M. T. "Free-lance Indexing." In *What Else You Can Do with a Library Degree,* ed. by Betty-Carol Sellen, pp. 138–146. Syracuse, N.Y.: Gaylord Professional Pubs., 1980. Individual example of experiences of a freelance indexer in New York.

Warner, A. S. "Information Services—New Use for an Old Product." *Wilson Library Bulletin* 49, no. 6 (February 1975): 440–444. Personal account of partnership and services offered by Warner-Eddison Associates in Massachusetts.

_____. "Noninstitutional Librarianship: Serving the Business Community." In *What Else You Can Do with a Library Degree,* ed. by Betty-Carol Sellen, pp. 29–34. Syracuse, N.Y.: Gaylord Professional Pubs., 1980. Description of beginnings of one company and how it has expanded.

Warnken, K. *The Directory of Fee-based Information Services: 1978–79.* Woodstock, N.Y.: Information Alternative, 1978. Comprehensive listing of fee-based information services, in private, public, and institutional libraries, in the United States and Canada. Provides name, address, telephone, key individuals, rates, services, areas of specialization, and further description for each entry. Annual.

————. *The Journal of Fee-Based Information Services.* Woodstock, N.Y.: Informative Alternative, bi-monthly.

Waterstreet, D. E. "Free-lance Information Management." In *What Else You Can Do with a Library Degree,* ed. by Betty-Carol Sellen, pp. 17–22. Syracuse, N.Y.: Gaylord Professional Pubs., 1980. The owner of Badger Infosearch describes her background and the advantages and disadvantages of freelancing from her own experiences.

Webb, T. "Alternative Careers: The Information Broker." *Footnotes* 10, no. 2 (January 1981): 1–2. Quick review of information brokerage business in the United States and writer's own company, Info Webb.

Weiner, B. "Free-lance Cataloging." In *What Else You Can Do with a Library Degree,* ed. by Betty-Carol Sellen, pp. 68–71. Syracuse, N.Y.: Gaylord Professional Pubs., 1980. Personal comments concerning requirements for freelancing, advertising, and charging practices.

INFORMATION INDUSTRY

AMERICAN

Berry, J. "Free Information and I.I.A." *Library Journal* 100, no. 9 (May 1, 1975): 795. Comment on a talk given by the executive director of IIA at the seventh annual meeting of the association. Calls for realization that public- and private-sector information activities should coexist.

Brinberg, H. R. "Information Industry." In *The ALA Yearbook 1980,* pp. 162–163. Chicago, Ill.: American Library Association, 1980. The decisions and activities of IIA in 1979. The information industry achieved maturity because it moved from a focus on definitional questions to more vital economic and societal questions.

Cuadra, C. "Information Industry." In *The ALA Yearbook 1977,* pp. 160–163. Chicago, Ill.: American Library Association, 1977. Full description of IIA and the variety of information products, systems, and services provided by its members.

Doebler, P. D. "Information Management: A Major New Discipline Comes of Age." *Publishers Weekly* 216, no. 8 (August 20, 1979): 39–40. The establishment of an organization for information managers called Associated Information Managers (AIM) and its goals.

————. "Order and Structure Emerging in Information Industry Activity." *Publishers Weekly* 203, no. 16 (April 16, 1973): 43–45. Good outline of types of information companies and a checklist of steps to go through to establish a small company.

_____. "Paul Zurkowski: The Head of the Information Industry." *Publishers Weekly* 203, no. 26 (June 25, 1973): 38–39. Opinions of role of IIA in American society and particularly in the information sector.

Emard, J. P. "N.I.C.E. III." *Bulletin of the American Society for Information Science* 5, no. 6 (August 1979): 22. Report of National Information Conference and Exposition sponsored by IIA with the theme of managing your information crisis: a multidisciplinary approach.

Farkas-Conn, I. S. "The Emerging Information Manager: A Challenge to ASIS." *Bulletin of the American Society for Information Science* 4, no. 5 (June 1978): 36. Discussion of the appearance of new organization called Program for Information Managers (PRIM) sponsored by IIA.

Gardner, R. J. "Is Tension Inevitable between S.L.A. and Associated Information Managers?" *Special libraries* 71, no. 9 (September 1980): 373–378. The relationship between special librarians and AIM, which demonstrates that an individual can benefit from both organizations.

Garfield, E. "Info-Expo/70: The Second Annual Meeting of the Information Industry Association." In *Essays of an Information Scientist*, vol. 1, 1962–1973, p. 93. Philadelphia, Pa.: I.S.I. Press, 1977. History and overall purpose of IIA.

"Information Industry Association Urges User Fees for Libraries in N.C.L.I.S. Testimony." *American libraries* 4, no. 6 (June 1973): 335. General statement by E. Garfield to the National Commission advocating user fees in libraries.

"The Information Industry: More Significant Than Ever." *Publishers Weekly* 201, no. 18 (May 1, 1972): 28–31. Report of the fourth annual meeting of IIA, which had emphasis on the development of an educated public for their products.

"Information Industry Promotes Libraries 'For-profit.' " *American Libraries* 4, no. 2 (February 1973): 79–80. A brief description of draft of statement circulated by IIA to its members before presentation to the National Commission on Libraries and Information Science.

"The 'Information' Market." *Publishers Weekly* 195, no. 15 (April 14, 1969): 64–67. Report of the first annual meeting of the newly organized IIA as a trade association designed to serve the interests of "private, for-profit information organizations" in the United States.

Jennings, M. S. "The Emerging Information Manager—Bridging the Gap." *Bulletin of the American Society for Information Science* 3, no. 4 (April 1977): 29–30. Report of the first National Information Conference and Exposition.

King, D. W. "N.I.C.E. II." *Bulletin of the American Society for Information Science* 4, no. 5 (June 1978): 28. Report of the second annual National Information Conference and Exposition, which included discussion of the new copyright law and the copyright clearance center.

Levitan, K. B. "Opportunities and Risks in the Information Business: The Next Ten Years." *Bulletin of the American Society of Information Science* 5, no. 3 (February 1979): 24–25. Report of the tenth annual meeting of IIA. Theme that information industries of all types need to work together as a whole.

Mount, E. "Information Industry Association." *Special libraries* 62, no. 7/8 (July/August 1971): 328. Account of a meeting between the Library Information Section of IIA and SLA librarians in New York City with the purpose of fostering better communication between the two groups.

Nyren, K. E. "The Information Communities." *Library Journal* 98, no. 9 (May 1, 1973): 1417. A short discussion of the place of IIA in the overall information community.

————. "Notes on a Triangle: The Second Information Industry Assn. Annual Meeting in Washington, D.C." *Library Journal* 95, no. 10 (May 15, 1970): 1803–1806. Conference had underlying theme of the relationship among three groups: for-profit firms, nonprofit organizations, and government agencies.

Pemberton, J. "I.I.A. Picture Story." *Online* 2, no. 3 (July 1978): 72–73. Collection of photos of second annual NICE.

————. "Online Goes to the I.I.A." *Online* 1, no. 3 (July 1977): 50–51. Photos and a short comment on 1977 I.I.A. annual conference.

Rugge, S., and Strauch, H. M. "I.I.A. Report." *Online* 2, no. 1 (January 1978): 53–54. Report of the ninth annual meeting of IIA, which focused on future directions of the industry.

Zurkowski, P. "Cost-effective Information." *Library Journal* 100, no. 11 (June 1, 1975): 1045. Role of IIA in issue of free-vs.-fee information in today's society.

————. "Information Industry." In *The ALA Yearbook 1978*, pp. 149–153. Chicago, Ill.: American Library Association, 1978. Major developments and important issues for IIA in 1977, especially emergence of information managers' own conference and special program (PRIM).

————. "Information Industry." In *The ALA Yearbook 1979*, pp. 131–135. Chicago, Ill.: American Library Association, 1979. Various steps taken by IIA in 1978 designed to expand its role as a major trade association in the nation's capital.

RELATED ITEMS

CANADA

Goodfellow, M. "Library Consulting: A View from Quebec." *Quebec Library Association Bulletin* 16, no. 2 (April–June 1975): 3–5. Definition of a library consultant; whether information consultants are needed in Canada.

Heaps, D. M., and Ingram, W. D. "Information Transfer in Canada: Position Paper: Background to Discussion." *(Proceedings of Fourth Annual Meeting.)* American Society for Information Sciences, Western Canada Chapter, pp. 171–181. Vancouver, B.C.: School of Librarianship, University of British Columbia, 1972. General discussion concerning information communication and transfer processes in Canada.

McMullen, R. M. "Information—Value and Cost." *Journal of the American Society for Information Science* 24, no. 5 (September–October 1973): 404. Letter to the editor giving personal opinion concerning the value of information—not as a free commodity but having certain costs.

Penner, R. J. "The Practice of Charging Users for Information Services: A State of the Art Report." *Journal of the American Society for Information Science* 21, no. 1 (January–February 1970): 67–74. State of the art literature review disclosed that society has not yet come to the point of paying for library information services as a common thing.

Schick, P. "Information for Sale." *Proceedings of the Seventh Annual Meeting*, American Society for Information Science, Western Canada Chapter, pp. 1–6. Edmonton, Alta.: The Library, University of Alberta, 1975. Examination of free-vs.-fee principle as it applies to information collection and distribution.

AMERICAN

Asp, W. G. "Search for Tomorrow: Or Facing New Information Needs without Tears." *Minnesota Libraries* 23, no. 11 (Autumn 1972): 316–322. Discussion of "tomorrow's" reference service and changes in technology. Development of community information centers proves the writer's forecasts true.

Berry, John, III, ed. *Directory of Library Consultants.* New York and London: R. R. Bowker Co., 1969. Provides a listing of active consultants in library and related professions in the United States.

Bevis, L. D. "The Librarian-Adventurers." In *What Else You Can Do with a Library Degree*, ed. by Betty-Carol Sellen, pp. 72–76. Syracuse, N.Y.: Gaylord Professional Pubs., 1980. A list of examples of librarians who have changed their focus within the library field.

Blake, F., and Perlmutter, E. "Libraries in the Marketplace." *Library Journal* 99, no. 2 (January 15, 1974): 108–111. An overview of all new terms being used and arguments in favor of user fees.

Doebler, P. "Profile of an 'Information Buyer.' " *Publishers Weekly* 204, no. 8 (August 20, 1973): 71–74. Focus on one special library and how people in business and professional life obtain information.

Garfield, E. "The Cost-effectiveness and Cost-benefits of Commercial Information Services." In *Essays of an Information Scientist*, vol. 2, 1974–1976, pp. 328–334. Philadelphia, Pa.: I.S.I. Press, 1977. Detailed discussion of aspects involved.

The Information Manager. Hempstead, N.Y., 1979–1981. Magazine of general information for information managers.

King, D. W., et al. "A National Profile of Information Professionals." *Bulletin of the American Society for Information Science* 6, no. 6 (August 1980): 18–22. Efforts to determine a precise definition of an information professional resulting in four generic categories and nine generic categories of functions performed.

Koger, E., and Puckett, K. "Setting Up a New Special Library." *Idaho Librarian* 29, no. 4 (October 1977): 156–159. Suggests steps to take if hired as a special librarian.

Lancaster, F. W. "Libraries and the Information Age." In *The ALA Yearbook 1980*, pp. 9–19. Chicago, Ill.: American Library Association, 1980. Consideration of all aspects of libraries in terms of the "information age" and a section on future professionals in private practices or information consulting companies.

Learmont, C. L. "Placements and Salaries 1979: Wider Horizons." *Library Journal* 105, no. 19 (November 1, 1980): 2271–2277. A survey in the United States and Canada, which includes information on the terms freelance, consulting, and information brokers, and comparative salary scales for all types of librarians.

Mason, E. E. "Library Consultants." *Library Trends*, Winter 1980. Whole issue devoted to the topic of library consultancy work, although emphasis not on freelancing.

Smith, J. I. "Marketing Information Products." In *Humanization of Knowledge in the Social Sciences—A Symposium*, ed. by P. Atherton, pp. 35–39. Syracuse, N.Y.: Syracuse University Press, 1972.

Stern, L. W., et al. "Promotion of Information Services: An Evaluation of Alternative Approaches." *Journal of the American Society for Information Science* 24, no. 3 (May–June 1973): 171–179. Access to information via computer-based information retrieval systems and promotion of it in libraries and the academic setting.

Steward, C. "The Expanding Job Market for Information Professionals." *Bulletin of the American Society for Information Science* 6, no. 1 (October 1979): 38–39. Types of background that information professionals have and therefore the types of services they can offer.

EDUCATIONAL ASPECTS

CANADIAN

Klement, S. "Draft Proposal for a Graduate Course on Alternatives in Librarianship." *Canadian Library Journal* 34, no. 2 (April 1977): 131–134. Detailed explanation for a graduate course, which could be used as a continuing education course as well.

AMERICAN

"Freelance Librarians." *Library Journal* 101, no. 5 (March 1, 1976): 653. Workshop on alternative information services held by Syracuse University School of Information Studies.

Hickey, D. J. "Room for Library Students?" *American Libraries* 5, no. 10 (November 1974): 527. Employment prospects for library graduates in the United States and the type of training that library school provides.

Roach, C. B. "Free-lancing Information—But Not for Free." *Bulletin of the American Society for Information Science* 3, no. 6 (August 1977): 16–17. Rationale for an area of concentration designed to prepare students for careers as consultants as part of the MLS program.

Smith, D. R. "Alternative Information Careers Eyed in Syracuse." *Library Journal* 102, no. 15 (September 1, 1977): 1712. Report of a workshop held at Syracuse University School of Information Studies, and the talks given by various speakers.

ITEMS OF INTEREST FROM OTHER COUNTRIES

AUSTRALIA

Symes, L. "Commercial and Freelance Library Services—Do They Have a Future?" In *Proceedings of the 18th Conference,* pp. 483–497. Melbourne, Vic.: Library Association of Australia, 1976. Overview of the historical development and use of these external services. Statement on future problems in the Australian context.

EUROPE

Stanfield, J. "Changes in the European Scene—Their Impact on the Market Place." In *The Marketing of Information Services,* ed. by M. Raffin, pp. 8–13. London: Aslib, 1978. Major forces affecting the European information marketplace.

SOUTH AFRICA

Bryer, V. "On Free-lancing in the Library World." *South African Libraries* 39, no. 2 (October 1971): 126–131. Total job description of a partnership of freelance librarians in South Africa.

UNITED KINGDOM

Davinson, D. "The Consultancy Racket." *New Library World* 73, no. 864 (June 1972): 318–319. The reasons for charging for services.

Hyams, M. "Information Science and the Profession of Communications." *Library Association Record* 82, no. 9 (September 1980): 397. The future of information science as a communications profession.

Offor, C. "Changing Patterns of Information." *Aslib Proceedings* 30, no. 1 (January 1978): 35–45. Good general discussion about information and society and the supply of information to users. Includes a discussion of information brokers and where they fit into the information network.

Saunders, W. L. "Information—The Unscarce Resource." *Library Association Record* 82, no. 9 (September 1980): 398–399. General discussion concerning the concept of information.

Usherwood, R. C. "Comment: Imposition of Direct User Charges Will Withdraw the Right to Information for Many Citizens." *Library Association Record* 80, no. 12 (December 1978): 601–602. Consideration of whether to charge for information services in libraries.

————. "Socio-economic Implications of the New Information Technology." *Aslib Proceedings* 32, no. 6 (June 1980): 276–278. Arguments for and against direct charges on users of public library services and the role of private information services.

White, M. S. "Information for Industry—The Role of the Information Broker." *Aslib Proceedings* 32, no. 2 (February 1980): 82–86. Information access for people in business and the role of the information broker in that system.

————. "Information Trader." *Library Review* 27 (Spring 1978): 4–6. Discusses problem of determining proper terminology and definition for role of information scientist.

Wilkin, A. "Some Comments on the Information Broker and the Technological Gatekeeper." *Aslib Proceedings* 26 (December 1974): 477–482. The relationship between the broker's role and the other information-handling roles in the English context.

INDEX